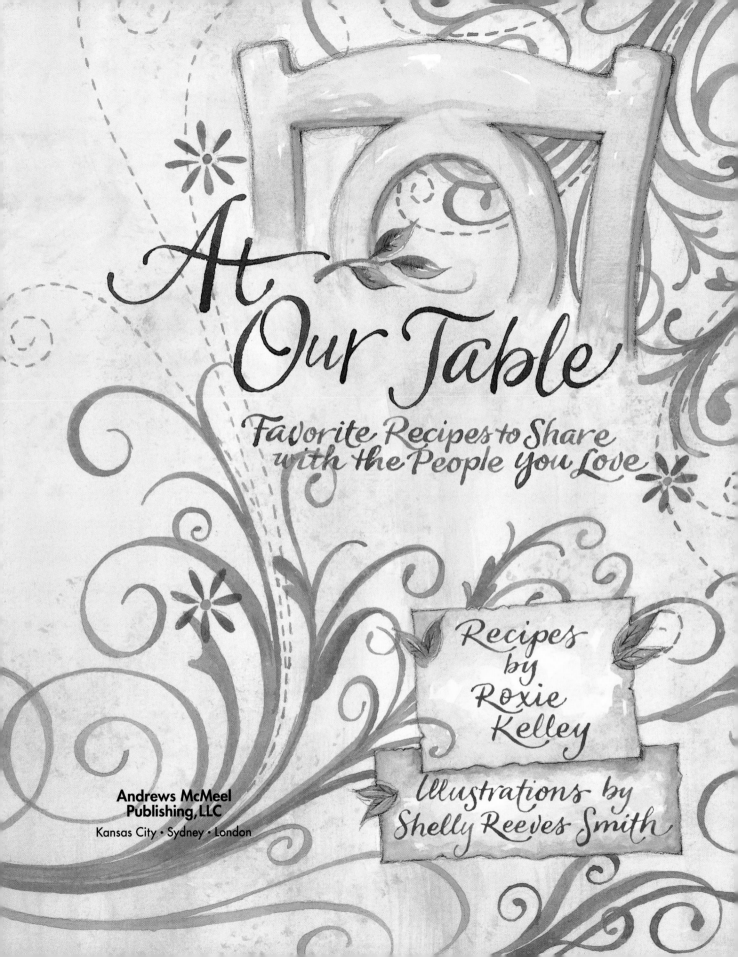

At Our Table

Favorite Recipes to Share with the People You Love

Recipes by Roxie Kelley

Illustrations by Shelly Reeves Smith

Andrews McMeel Publishing, LLC

Kansas City • Sydney • London

At Our Table copyright © 2010 by Roxie Kelley. Illustrations © 2010 by Shelly Reeves Smith. All rights reserved. Printed in China. No part of this book may be used or reproduced in any manner whatsoever without written permission except in the case of reprints in the context of reviews. For information, write Andrews McMeel Publishing, LLC, an Andrews McMeel Universal company, 1130 Walnut Street, Kansas City, Missouri 64106.

10 11 12 13 14 WKT 10 9 8 7 6 5 4 3 2 1

ISBN-13: 978-0-7407-8346-3
ISBN-10: 0-7407-8346-7

Library of Congress Control Number: 2009938773

www.andrewsmcmeel.com

ATTENTION: SCHOOLS AND BUSINESSES
Andrews McMeel books are available at quantity discounts with bulk purchase for educational, business, or sales promotional use. For information, please write to: Special Sales Department, Andrews McMeel Publishing, LLC, 1130 Walnut Street, Kansas City, Missouri 64106.

Presented To:

To Kim —
We look forward to sharing
with you the table He has
prepared for us.
Psalm 23: 1–6
With love,
Blake, Brooke, and Roxie

To my dad, Tom Reeves —
For teaching me to find art in words.
Love, Shelly

Contents

Dear Friends
xi

Ingredients
xiii

Appetizers

Main Dishes

Side Dishes and Salads

Breads, Muffins & Spreads

Desserts

Ihis
and That

Dear Friends,

Because I am a person who really responds to color and light, I consider it such an honor to have my thoughts and recipes sharing the same page with the incredible art of Shelly Reeves Smith, my friend of more than 30 years. Thank you for your continued interest in our work and for sharing it with the people who gather at _your_ table.

When I first broke the news of another book to my family, they reacted with a fist-pumping "Yes!" I understood in that moment how limited my cooking had become and how much my family had missed that feeling of abundance that an active kitchen creates.

How and when did it happen — that wide circle I walked around the kitchen? Blake (my son) was away at college and we had a busy calendar with Brooke's (my daughter) sports schedule. Lately, it felt like I didn't have enough time in between all the scheduled events to put a real meal on the table. This was one of my excuses, along with, "If I cook a big meal today, when would we even be home to eat the left-overs?" Haven't you had similar questions floating around inside your head regarding your meal planning?

And yet, every time we sacrificed "table-time" together, it seemed as if those grab-and-go meals were draining us of our energy and enthusiasm, instead of lifting us to a higher and healthier place. But as we all know, one day at a time we give those days away, until they become years given away.

So, in the middle of the creation of this book, I saw that I _did_ have enough time to be in my kitchen. And I did have the resources to create fun meals to share with the people I love. I also discovered that we enjoyed more family time when we prepared meals together. I found that gathering for meals around our table energized all of us and helped us to see how full and rich our lives were. I wanted to continue to approach mealtime with this attitude — we have _more than enough_ of everything we need, and _we have today_.

Perhaps you'll find what I am discovering in this process. Abundance is all around us. It's not always a tangible thing. We have found not only an abundance of food and the time to prepare it but also wisdom, joy, encouragement, and grace. All of these things are around our table, waiting for us to acknowledge them. This book is about that kind of abundance.

My hope is that, as you use this book and spend more time in your kitchen, you'll discover that your "cup runneth over" in all these ways and more.

And now I wish you more abundant time at your table,

Roxie Kelley

Ingredients

Our readers seem so appreciative of the fact that most of the ingredients listed in our books are fairly easy to find. We live in a resort area that is really just a group of small towns surrounding a big lake. So I completely understand how difficult it might be if you live in a remote area to find what you need to prepare a recipe.

Below are brief descriptions of some of the basic ingredients used throughout this book.

Butter: It might be helpful for you, as you begin using <u>At Our Table</u>, to know that I don't mention in any of my recipes whether to use unsalted or salted butter. Most cookbooks suggest using unsalted butter, permitting the cook to have more control over the salt content of the recipe. This is particularly helpful when you are preparing food for someone on a low-salt diet. But to be honest, I always use salted butter. I just prefer the taste, and I've never pushed myself to make a change in the way I cook. So keep that in mind as you prepare these recipes.

Eggs: Use large eggs for the best results. I have variously used low-cholesterol eggs or regular eggs in my recipes, and I have not noticed any difference at all in the flavor or texture of the final prepared dishes.

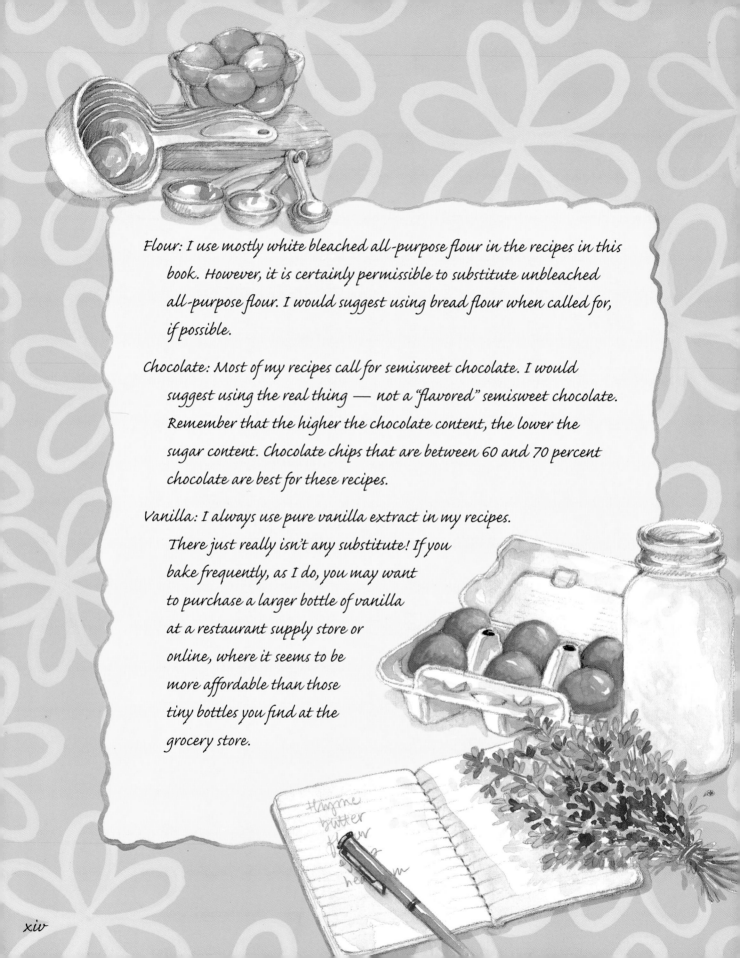

Flour: I use mostly white bleached all-purpose flour in the recipes in this book. However, it is certainly permissible to substitute unbleached all-purpose flour. I would suggest using bread flour when called for, if possible.

Chocolate: Most of my recipes call for semisweet chocolate. I would suggest using the real thing — not a "flavored" semisweet chocolate. Remember that the higher the chocolate content, the lower the sugar content. Chocolate chips that are between 60 and 70 percent chocolate are best for these recipes.

Vanilla: I always use pure vanilla extract in my recipes. There just really isn't any substitute! If you bake frequently, as I do, you may want to purchase a larger bottle of vanilla at a restaurant supply store or online, where it seems to be more affordable than those tiny bottles you find at the grocery store.

Appetizers

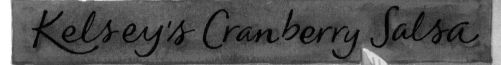

Kelsey's Cranberry Salsa

Kelsey Adams is one of those remarkable young ladies who is power-packed with giftedness. She coaches, she teaches, she creates, and she even cooks! Here is her fun and fruity salsa recipe — you're going to love this.

12 ounces fresh or frozen cranberries, chopped
1 Granny Smith apple, cored and chopped
½ red bell pepper, seeded and chopped
½ medium red onion, chopped
3 tablespoons chopped fresh cilantro
2 tablespoons pickled jalapeño peppers
¾ cup sugar
⅓ cup apple juice
Tortilla chips, for serving

Mix all the ingredients, except for the tortilla chips, in a medium bowl. Cover and refrigerate overnight. Serve with tortilla chips of your choice. This will keep in the refrigerator for 2 weeks.

Makes about 4 cups

Black Bean and Corn Salsa

I adore this salsa — and it's really very good for you! How could you ask for more, right?

1 cup frozen corn, thawed

1 (15-ounce) can black beans, rinsed and drained

1 cup seeded chopped tomatoes

½ cup chopped green onions

2 or 3 serrano chiles

2 tablespoons chopped fresh cilantro

3 tablespoons olive oil

2 tablespoons freshly squeezed lemon juice

1 teaspoon ground cumin

Salt and freshly ground black pepper

Tortilla chips, for serving

Combine the corn, black beans, tomatoes, onions, serranos, and cilantro in a medium bowl. In a small bowl, whisk together the oil, lemon juice, and cumin. Season with salt and pepper. Pour the dressing over the corn mixture and toss until well combined. Cover and refrigerate overnight to allow the flavors to blend. Serve with your favorite tortilla chips. This will keep in the refrigerator for 2 weeks.

Serves 4–6

Cheryl's Cucumber-Tomato Salsa

I enjoyed this at the home of my friend, Cheryl Castle. She served it with her Hummus Spread with Pita Bread (page 6). It was so yummy. Cheryl suggests serving this dish as soon as it has had a chance to chill, rather than preparing it in advance.

¼ cup freshly squeezed lemon juice

2 tablespoons olive oil

½ teaspoon salt

¼ teaspoon freshly ground black pepper

2 cloves garlic, minced

4 cups seeded, chopped tomatoes

2 cups seeded, chopped cucumber

⅓ cup loosely packed thinly sliced green onion tops

¼ cup loosely packed chopped fresh parsley

1 tablespoon chopped fresh cilantro

Tortilla chips, for serving

Combine all of the ingredients, except for the tortilla chips, in a medium bowl. Cover and chill for about 20 minutes before serving with the chips. This will keep in the refrigerator for 1 week.

Serves 6–8

A Little Gift of Herbs

This mix makes a great party favor when packaged in small cellophane bags or plastic containers. Write the recipe for Herb Cheese Spread (page 7) on a small card and tie it to the package with a ribbon.

1 teaspoon garlic powder

2 teaspoons dried oregano

1 teaspoon dried dill weed

1 teaspoon dried marjoram

1 teaspoon dried basil

1 teaspoon dried thyme

2 teaspoons freshly ground black pepper

Combine all of the ingredients in a small bowl and blend with a wire whisk. Store in an airtight container or bag until ready for use or gift giving. It will keep for up to 6 months.

Makes 3 tablespoons

Recipe: _Hummus Spread with Pita Bread_   **From:** _Cheryl_

This is also a recipe from Cheryl Castle. I'm embarrassed to admit this, but hummus always sounded like something too healthy for me to enjoy. Cheryl's recipe helped rid me of that notion, and I've been partaking ever since.

1 (15-ounce) can chickpeas, drained (reserve ½ cup of the liquid)

½ cup tahini (sesame paste)

3 tablespoons freshly squeezed lemon juice

¼ cup chopped yellow onion

3 cloves garlic, chopped

2 teaspoons olive oil

⅛ teaspoon ground red pepper

Pinch of salt

1 (11-ounce) package pita bread

Olive oil

French gray sea salt

Puree the chickpeas (without the reserved liquid), tahini, lemon juice, onion, garlic, olive oil, red pepper, and salt together in a food processor or blender. Slowly add the reserved liquid as needed to reach the desired consistency. Refrigerate for at least 4 hours.

When ready to serve, preheat the oven to 425°F.

Place the pita bread on a baking sheet. Brush each piece lightly with olive oil. Sprinkle a conservative amount of sea salt on each piece. Bake for 5–6 minutes, or until lightly browned but not crispy. Cut each pita into 6 wedges and serve with hummus.

Note: Cheryl suggests serving Cucumber-Tomato Salsa (page 4) on the side.

Makes 1¾ cups

Herb Cheese Spread

This is such a versatile spread that you may want to keep a batch of it on hand on a regular basis. It has a rich but mellow flavor and tastes as good on a cracker as it does blended into other recipes (see Herbed Potato Gratin, page 75).

¼ cup butter, softened
1 (8-ounce) package cream cheese, softened
1 tablespoon A Little Gift of Herbs (page 5)

Using a standing mixer with a paddle attachment, blend the butter and cream cheese together until smooth, about 1 minute. Add the seasoning and mix well. Cover and store in the refrigerator until ready to serve. This will keep in the refrigerator for up to 1 month.

Makes 2½ cups

Jody's Feta Cheese Spread

Thank you to Jody Welsh, a good friend and respected teacher in our community, for sharing this rich and tangy recipe.

4 ounces crumbled feta cheese

4 ounces cream cheese, softened

⅓ cup mayonnaise

¼ teaspoon crushed dried basil

¼ teaspoon crushed dried oregano

⅛ teaspoon dried dill weed

⅛ teaspoon dried thyme

Assorted fresh vegetables, for dipping

Crackers or toasted slices of French bread, for serving

Using a fork, mix the cheeses, mayonnaise, and herbs together in a small bowl until smooth. Serve with the vegetables and crackers or bread.

Makes 1⅓ cups

Mexicorn Dip

This recipe came by way of Susan Brown, with a little note in the margin that said, "This is really Paula Brackett's recipe!" So, that being said, my whole family wants to thank both of these friends for sharing this recipe with us. My favorite things about this dish: 1) you can assemble it in less than 5 minutes, 2) it tastes so fresh, and 3) it's so much more substantial than the typical "chip dip." Mexicorn is a fun blend of corn and peppers and can be found in the same section as plain canned corn in your grocery store.

2 (11-ounce) cans Mexicorn, drained

1 cup sour cream

1 cup mayonnaise

1 bunch green onion tops, sliced

3–4 tablespoons chopped pickled jalapeño peppers

1 pound shredded Cheddar-Jack cheese blend

Garlic salt

Corn chips or tortilla chips, for serving

Mix all the ingredients, except for the garlic salt and chips, in a medium bowl and season with garlic salt to taste. Cover and chill until ready to serve. This will keep in the refrigerator for up to 1 week. Serve with corn chips or tortilla chips on the side.

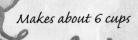

Makes about 6 cups

Peppercorn Dip

This is a simple but snappy dip that can be prepared in less than 5 minutes. I predict you're going to love this. I like grinding a medley of different peppercorns for this recipe. Look in the spice aisle of your grocery store for a combination of black, pink, white, and green peppercorns.

2 (8-ounce) packages cream cheese, softened
½ cup butter, softened
1 (1-ounce) package ranch dip mix
½ cup grated Parmesan cheese
Freshly ground pepper
Pretzels, pretzel chips, and/or crackers, for dipping

Using a standing mixer with a paddle attachment, blend the cream cheese, butter, dip mix, and Parmesan cheese until smooth, about 1 minute. Spread in a shallow serving dish and cover generously with pepper. Serve at room temperature with pretzels or crackers.

Makes 4 cups

Kelly's Tutti Fruity Dip

Tutti frutti is an Italian phrase meaning "all fruits," and this dip recipe certainly works with any and all fruits. My friend Kelly Garr serves the dip inside the hollowed-out lower half of a pineapple to add a little tropical flair. This recipe fits Kelly's personality — bright, beautiful, and consistently fun!

1 (10-ounce) jar lemon curd

⅓ cup sweetened condensed milk

¼ cup half-and-half

Lemon zest, for garnish

1 fresh pineapple, cut into bite-size pieces, for serving

2 pints strawberries, washed and stemmed, for serving

3 apples, peeled, cored, and sliced, for serving

In a medium bowl, using a wire whisk, blend the lemon curd with the sweetened condensed milk and half-and-half until smooth. Transfer the mixture into a serving dish (or into the bottom of the pineapple as noted above) and garnish with the lemon zest. Arrange the fruit on a pretty platter and serve.

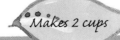
Makes 2 cups

Joy's Glazed Pecans

One of our designers at a store I used to own is responsible for our entire staff falling in love with this treat. Thank you, Joy, for sharing all of your gifts, including this recipe.

2 egg whites
1 tablespoon salt
8 cups pecans (about 2 pounds)
1½ cups sugar
2 teaspoons ground cinnamon

Preheat the oven to 225°F. Line two baking sheets with parchment paper.

Beat the egg whites and salt in a small bowl with a whisk until thick and frothy. Put the nuts in a large bowl, pour the egg whites over the nuts, and mix well. Combine the sugar and cinnamon in a separate bowl and add to the nuts. Mix well and transfer onto the prepared pans. Bake for 1 hour, stirring every 15 minutes. Cool completely before storing in an airtight container. This will keep for up to 1 month.

Makes 8 cups

Kate and Maureen's Pinwheel Re-Treats

I gave this appetizer this particular name because I like to imagine my special friends, Kate and Maureen (mother and daughter), preparing them at their family lakeside retreat in Innsbrook, Missouri. A few years ago when Kate and Tom Gunn decided to purchase a piece of property in this spectacular resort area, they called me and asked if I might be interested in helping them design their home there. Working with the Gunns on such a project was not like work at all. I can't even begin to describe what a privilege this was. The Gunn family's love has overflowed on me and I count myself blessed to know them.

1 (8-ounce) package refrigerated crescent roll dough
3 ounces cream cheese, softened
1 (2.8-ounce) package real bacon bits
2 tablespoons onion flakes
1 cup grated Parmesan cheese

Preheat the oven to 350°F. Coat two baking sheets with nonstick cooking spray.

Unroll the dough and separate into 4 rectangles. Firmly press the perforations together to seal. Layer each rectangle with cream cheese, bacon bits, and onion flakes. Starting with the short side, roll up each rectangle. Press the edges to seal. With a serrated knife, cut each roll into 6 equal slices. Roll each slice in the Parmesan cheese. Transfer the slices to the prepared baking sheets. Bake for 15 minutes or until the edges are slightly brown. Serve warm.

Makes 24 treats

Chick-a-Dillies

Shelly's friend Susanna learned to make this appetizer from her mother, Ruth. They were originally called Mini Chicken Turnovers, but Susanna and her sisters gave them this kid-friendly name — fitting for a treat just the right size for a child's hands.

Filling
3 tablespoons chopped yellow onion

3 tablespoons butter

1¾ cups shredded cooked chicken

3 tablespoons chicken broth

1 clove garlic, minced

Salt

¼ teaspoon poultry seasoning

3 ounces cream cheese, cubed

Pastry
1½ cups all-purpose flour

½ teaspoon paprika

½ teaspoon salt

½ cup cold butter

Preheat the oven to 375°F.

For the filling, in a large skillet, sauté the onion in the butter until tender. Stir in the chicken, chicken broth, garlic, salt, and poultry seasoning. Add the cream cheese and blend well. Set aside.

For the pastry, combine the flour, paprika, and salt in a medium bowl. Cut in the butter until the mixture resembles coarse crumbs. Gradually add enough water to make a stiff dough. On a floured surface, roll out the pastry to a 1/16-inch thickness. Cut with a 2½-inch round cutter. Repeat until all the dough is cut.

Mound a heaping teaspoon of filling on half of each circle. Fold the dough in half over the filling and crimp the edges closed with a fork. Transfer each turnover to an ungreased baking sheet. Prick the tops with a fork. Bake for 15–20 minutes, until golden brown. Turnovers can be baked, frozen for up to 2 months, and reheated at 375°F for 5–7 minutes.

Makes about 2 dozen

Auntie's Pretzels

Here is a clone of that famous pretzel I can hardly ever resist when we're doing our "day at the mall" shopping. It took a lot of practice to get comfortable with the twisting of the dough to create the traditional knotted pretzel. But even if they look a little rustic compared to the chain variety, they still taste great. Have fun with this one!

1½ cups warm water

2 (¼-ounce) packages quick-rise yeast

2 tablespoons brown sugar

1½ teaspoons salt

1 cup bread flour

3–4 cups all-purpose flour

Baking Soda Bath

2 tablespoons baking soda

2 cups warm water

¼ cup butter, melted, for serving

Sea salt, for serving

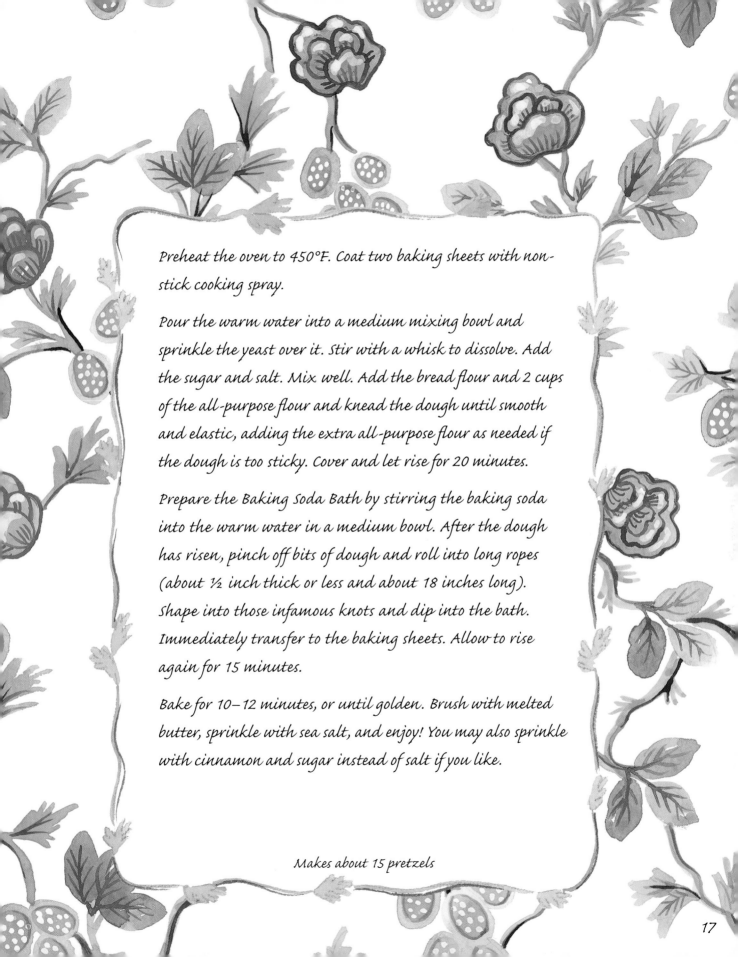

Preheat the oven to 450°F. Coat two baking sheets with non-stick cooking spray.

Pour the warm water into a medium mixing bowl and sprinkle the yeast over it. Stir with a whisk to dissolve. Add the sugar and salt. Mix well. Add the bread flour and 2 cups of the all-purpose flour and knead the dough until smooth and elastic, adding the extra all-purpose flour as needed if the dough is too sticky. Cover and let rise for 20 minutes.

Prepare the Baking Soda Bath by stirring the baking soda into the warm water in a medium bowl. After the dough has risen, pinch off bits of dough and roll into long ropes (about ½ inch thick or less and about 18 inches long). Shape into those infamous knots and dip into the bath. Immediately transfer to the baking sheets. Allow to rise again for 15 minutes.

Bake for 10–12 minutes, or until golden. Brush with melted butter, sprinkle with sea salt, and enjoy! You may also sprinkle with cinnamon and sugar instead of salt if you like.

Makes about 15 pretzels

Doo Dah Doodles

Rather than purchasing expensive snack mixes, try creating your own using this recipe. Send a batch of this on the bus with your church or sports camp kids!

1 (10-ounce) box miniature butter crackers

1 (10-ounce) box miniature pretzels

1 (10-ounce) box thin wheat crackers

1½ cups nuts (such as almonds, cashews, or pecans)

1 (1-ounce) package ranch dressing mix

1½ teaspoons garlic salt

⅔ cup vegetable oil

Preheat the oven to 200°F. Line two baking sheets with parchment paper.

Combine all the ingredients, except for the vegetable oil, in a large bowl and mix. Pour the oil evenly over all and stir gently to combine. Divide the mixture evenly between the baking sheets and bake for 30 minutes, stirring halfway through the baking time. Let cool, and store in an airtight container. This will keep for up to 1 month.

Makes 14 cups

Table Topics

A very long time ago (before marriage and children) I owned a little café in a resort area in Missouri. Every August I would take a day trip for research. I would go out of town and visit four or five restaurants, ordering an appetizer here, a dessert there. My goals were to try and gain a new perspective, get an objective view of my own restaurant, and grade "us against them." It was very helpful for my business, but there was also a personal bonus lesson for me in the experience.

My bonus was an increased awareness (as I dined alone) of how many couples and families sat at the same table together and had absolutely nothing to say to one another. I suppose this was also happening in my own establishment, but in my own business I was too busy seating guests, and assisting the waitstaff and people in the kitchen, to notice what was happening between guests once I got them to their table.

This awareness frightened me a little. I wondered, if I got married and had a family, would we end up like that — gazing off into space, looking like we were completely bored with the company of those people who were supposed to mean the most to us? I also thought, How did that happen to them? Surely there must have been a time in their relationships when one had something to say that the other deemed worth listening to. Were the teenagers thinking, I'd rather be anywhere else but here, with anyone else but them! And if they were, how could I keep that from happening in my future family?

And that is how I came to value the fine art of dinner conversation and good table manners. I started thinking of little games I could play at the dinner table with my future mate and "someday children" that would keep pleasant conversation second nature. After marriage and children, it became a fun challenge for me to create different ways I could ensure my family knew how to engage with others in a positive and respectful way. Blake and Brooke's dad added so much to this experience. He always had a funny anecdote to share and was committed to teaching the children good table manners. Our table was "fight-free," full of kind or humorous interchanges, and really fun most of the time. And to this day, my children never leave the table without saying, "Thank you for dinner, Mom." Their father passed away several years ago, but I just know this simple expression of their gratitude is, even now, music to his ears as well as mine.

Thanks for dinner, Mom

Main Dishes

Grilled Cheese Dippers

"The Baker Girls," as they are known in our community, are my children's closest friends. My children, Blake and Brooke, hardly know how to celebrate a major holiday without Whitney, Blaire, and Haley. Needless to say, we have shared countless meals together. So when they heard I was in major testing mode for this book, they invited us to lunch to experience firsthand the recipes they wanted to submit.

Among the many wonderful dishes they served to us that day was this recipe. If you prepare the Grilled Cheese Dippers with the Southwestern Tomato-Cheese Soup on page 24, you'll have just a little taste of the kind of heaven these girls have brought into our lives. We love you, Baker Girls.

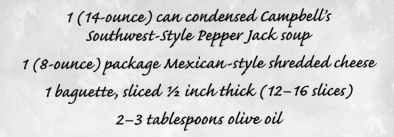

1 (14-ounce) can condensed Campbell's
Southwest-Style Pepper Jack soup
1 (8-ounce) package Mexican-style shredded cheese
1 baguette, sliced ½ inch thick (12–16 slices)
2–3 tablespoons olive oil

Preheat the oven to 200°F. You will not be baking the sandwiches, but you might want to keep the sandwiches in the warm oven until you are ready to serve them.

In a medium bowl, combine the soup and shredded cheese. Spread this mixture on the bread slices. Assemble 2 of the slices together, with the cheese mixture in the middle, to make a small sandwich. Brush each side of the sandwiches with the olive oil.

Heat a heavy skillet or griddle over medium-high heat. You may also use a panini grill if you have one. Place the sandwiches in the skillet and cook until golden brown on one side, about 2 minutes. Turn the sandwiches over and cook for another 2 minutes.

Keep the sandwiches warm in the oven until ready to serve.

Makes 6–8 servings

Southwestern Tomato~Cheese Soup

You'll want to take a look at the Grilled Cheese Dippers recipe on the previous page if you haven't already, and consider serving this soup with them on the side. Guests can make the soup even spicier if they want by adding a dash of Tabasco sauce.

1 (14-ounce) can condensed tomato soup
1 (14-ounce) can condensed Cheddar cheese soup
3 cups spicy tomato juice
1 teaspoon dried basil

Combine all the ingredients in a medium saucepan. Heat thoroughly, over medium heat, stirring occasionally. Serve hot.

Makes 6–8 servings

Pretzel Dogs

These are just plain fun. It doesn't matter how old you are. It doesn't even matter that hot dogs may not be one of your top fifty favorite foods. Just do this some Sunday afternoon and I promise you, it will be one of your most memorable meals for a very long time.

½ the dough recipe from Auntie's Pretzels (page 16)
8 all-beef hot dogs
Sea salt
Your favorite condiments, for serving

Preheat the oven to 375°F. Coat a large baking sheet with nonstick cooking spray.

Using about half of the dough, make 8 ropes about ½ inch in diameter and 10 inches long. Dip the ropes, one at a time, into the baking soda bath. Wrap each rope around a hot dog on an angle, tucking the ends under the hot dog as you lay it on the baking sheet. Sprinkle each with sea salt. Leave 2 inches between each pretzel dog. Let them rest for 15 minutes.

Bake for 14–16 minutes, or until golden brown. Serve warm with your favorite condiments.

Makes 8 servings

Baked Mostaccioli

This is another recipe for which my friend Kelly Garr is almost famous! She prepares this pasta dish for friends in need (new babies in the house, family emergencies, etc.). Everyone raves!

1 (1-pound) package mostaccioli
Salt
1 tablespoon minced garlic
1 pound Italian sausage
1 (14-ounce) can tomato sauce

1 (2-ounce) package spaghetti
    sauce seasoning
1 (16-ounce) jar Alfredo sauce
2 cups shredded mozzarella cheese

Preheat the oven to 350°F. Coat a 9 by 13-inch baking dish with nonstick cooking spray.

Prepare the pasta according to the package directions, adding the salt and garlic to the water in which the pasta is cooking. Drain and set aside.

Brown the sausage in a heavy skillet over medium-high heat. Remove from the heat and drain the sausage on paper towels.

In a large bowl, combine the sausage, tomato sauce, seasoning, and Alfredo sauce. Spoon half of the pasta into the bottom of the baking dish. Follow with half of the meat sauce. Sprinkle 1 cup of the cheese over the meat sauce. Repeat each layer, ending with the cheese. Bake for 30 minutes or until the cheese is melted and bubbly.

Makes 6–8 servings

Grilled Pepper Steaks

Begin by preparing this recipe the night before, since you'll want the steaks to marinate overnight. Because you'll be serving the steaks sliced, the addition of a variety of roasted vegetables to your menu will stretch this dish nicely among many guests.

¾ cup olive oil

⅓ cup soy sauce

¼ cup Dijon mustard

4 cloves garlic, minced

1 teaspoon sea salt

Coarsely ground black pepper

2 (1-pound) flank steaks

Whisk the oil, soy sauce, mustard, garlic, salt, and pepper together until well blended. Place the steaks in a single layer in a large baking dish. Pour the marinade over the meat and turn to coat. Cover and refrigerate overnight.

Heat the grill to medium.

Remove the steaks from the marinade. Discard the marinade. Season both sides generously with more pepper. Grill the steaks for 4–6 minutes per side to reach medium-rare to medium doneness. Let the steaks rest for a few minutes before slicing diagonally across the grain. Arrange the slices on a platter to serve.

Makes 6–8 servings

Chicken with Pasta

You can substitute cooked turkey for the chicken in this recipe with equally tasty results.

8 ounces white mushrooms, sliced

¼ cup butter

1 (10¾-ounce) can cream of mushroom soup

½ cup half-and-half

2 tablespoons white wine or chicken broth

2 cups cooked diced chicken

8 ounces penne pasta, cooked according to package directions

½ cup grated Parmesan cheese

Preheat the oven to 375°F. Grease a 2-quart casserole dish.

In a medium skillet, sauté the mushrooms in the butter over medium heat. Combine the soup, half-and-half, and wine in a large bowl until well blended. Add the chicken, pasta, and mushrooms and mix gently. Spread the mixture in the prepared dish. Top with the cheese and bake for 25 minutes.

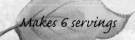

Makes 6 servings

Crispy Baked Tilapia

Our whole family loves this dish. And for that reason, it's one of my very favorites. Isn't it a good feeling when everyone leaves the table satisfied but not stuffed? A little bit of bliss!

1 pound tilapia fillets

¾ cup butter, melted

18 butter-flavored crackers, crushed

½ cup dry bread crumbs

1 teaspoon freshly squeezed lemon juice

½ cup grated Parmesan cheese

Salt and freshly ground black pepper

Preheat the oven to 450°F. Place the fish in a 9 by 13-inch baking dish.

Combine the butter, cracker crumbs, bread crumbs, lemon juice, cheese, and salt and pepper in a medium bowl. Mix well and spread this mixture over the fish. Bake for 18–20 minutes, or until golden brown.

Makes 4 servings

HAWAIIAN CHICKEN

One January, my son and daughter and I went to Hawaii for a little vacation. We had never ventured that far from home before, and we looked forward to a week of golf and fun in the sun. What a gift it was, to have this time together in such a beautiful place. Of course we ate fresh pineapple every single day, sometimes several times a day. This chicken dish is a sweet reminder of that special week away. It goes well with Macadamia Wild Rice Pilaf (page 74).

Vegetable oil, for frying
4 boneless, skinless chicken breasts
1 egg, slightly beaten
1 cup Bread Crumb Blend (page 146)
1 teaspoon salt
1 cup pineapple juice
2 tablespoons freshly squeezed lemon or orange juice
1 tablespoon cornstarch
1 tablespoon sugar
1 cup canned pineapple tidbits

Pour enough oil in a heavy frying pan to cover the bottom and heat over medium-high heat. Dip each chicken breast into the beaten egg, then dredge each side in the Bread Crumb Blend. Season with the salt. Carefully place the chicken in the hot oil and fry on each side until golden brown. Remove the chicken from the heat and place on paper towels to drain excess oil.

Lower the heat under the skillet to low. Combine the fruit juices, cornstarch, and sugar in a container with a lid and shake until mixed well. Pour this mixture into the skillet containing the oil and blend well. Stir over low heat for 1 minute.

Return the chicken to the pan with the thickening juice. Cover and let simmer for 20 minutes. Transfer the chicken and sauce to a platter and top with the pineapple pieces.

Makes 4 servings

Brooke's Baja Tacos

My daughter, Brooke, prepared these tacos for us one evening this summer. They were so light and delicious! Brooke loves to experiment with recipes containing fresh fruit, so she combined some of her favorites to create the salsa served with these tacos. You can substitute grilled chicken for the fish if you like for an equally tasty meal.

1–2 pounds tilapia fillets

2 tablespoons olive oil

2 teaspoons ground cumin

2 teaspoons chili powder

1 teaspoon freshly ground black pepper

1–2 teaspoons sea salt

Cilantro Cream

¼ cup light mayonnaise

¼ cup light sour cream

2 tablespoons freshly squeezed lime juice

2 tablespoons chopped fresh cilantro

Avocado-Orange Salsa

2–3 medium oranges, peeled and diced (no white pith, please!)

2 avocados, pitted, peeled, and diced

½ cup diced red onion

2 cloves garlic, minced

Grated peel and juice of 2 limes

2 tablespoons olive oil

1 tablespoon chopped fresh cilantro

½ teaspoon ground cumin

½ teaspoon sea salt

4–6 large flour tortillas

1 cup shredded lettuce

Brush both sides of the tilapia with 1 tablespoon of the olive oil. Combine the cumin, chili powder, pepper, and salt in a small dish and then sprinkle evenly over both sides of each fillet. Heat the remaining 1 tablespoon of oil in a large skillet over medium-high heat. Add the fish to the skillet and cook until lightly browned and flaking easily with a fork, about 3 minutes per side. Separate into bite-size pieces.

To prepare the Cilantro Cream, combine all the ingredients in a small bowl and blend until smooth.

To prepare the Avocado-Orange Salsa, combine all the ingredients in a medium bowl and stir gently.

Assemble by spreading each tortilla with the Cilantro Cream, topping it with some of the fish and the Avocado-Orange Salsa, and finishing with the lettuce.

Makes 4 servings

Slow-Cooker Pork Chops

Invest just 15 minutes in the morning putting this recipe together and you will be rewarded with the comforting aroma of an almost complete dinner when you arrive home that evening! Special thanks to Tim and Kelsey Adams for sharing this recipe.

2 tablespoons vegetable oil

⅓ cup all-purpose flour

1 teaspoon garlic salt

Freshly ground black pepper

1 teaspoon dry mustard

4–6 lean pork chops

1 (14-ounce) can cream of chicken soup

Warm the oil in a heavy skillet over medium-high heat.

Combine the flour, garlic salt, pepper, and dry mustard in a shallow dish. Dredge the chops in this mixture, coating both sides. Carefully place the chops in the hot oil and brown for 2 minutes on each side.

Remove the chops from the oil and place in a slow cooker. Pour the soup over the chops. Cover with the lid and cook on the low setting for 6–8 hours.

Makes 4–6 servings

Slow-Cooker Ribs

I have never had such tender ribs! And what a bonus — to be able to leave in the morning (after only 15 minutes of prep work) and return home to this tasty dish.

1 tablespoon minced onion

1 teaspoon crushed red pepper flakes

½ teaspoon ground cinnamon

1 teaspoon garlic powder

3 pounds pork loin back ribs, cut into serving-size pieces

1 medium yellow onion, sliced

½ cup water

1 cup barbecue sauce

In a small bowl, combine the minced onion, red pepper flakes, cinnamon, and garlic powder. Rub this mixture into the ribs on both sides.

Layer the ribs with the onion slices in a slow cooker. Pour the water around the ribs. Cover and cook on the low setting for 8–9 hours. One hour before serving, remove the ribs from the slow cooker. Dispose of the liquid and onion and return the ribs to the slow cooker. Pour the barbecue sauce over the ribs. Cover and continue cooking on low for another hour.

Makes 4–6 servings

White Bean Chili

My neighbors at Mystic Bay, Debbie and Keith, shared this fun chili recipe. It's a beautiful, confetti-like concoction, just full of goodness! Bake some big, mouthwatering corn muffins to serve with Beehive Butter (page 87) on the side.

1 tablespoon olive oil

1 medium yellow onion, chopped

¼ cup finely chopped carrots

4 cloves garlic, minced

1 (10-ounce) can RO-TEL tomatoes, drained

1 teaspoon ground cumin

¼ teaspoon cayenne pepper

½ teaspoon ground oregano

¼ teaspoon ground cloves

4 boneless, skinless chicken breasts,
grilled, and cut into 1-inch pieces

1 (32-ounce) jar great Northern beans, rinsed and drained

4 cups chicken broth

5 cups shredded Monterey Jack cheese

2 cups sour cream, for serving (optional)

In a large pot, heat the olive oil over medium heat. Add the onion, carrots, garlic, tomatoes, cumin, cayenne pepper, oregano, and cloves. Sauté for 3–5 minutes. Add the chicken, beans, and chicken broth. Lower the heat and simmer for 20 minutes. Add 3 cups of the Monterey Jack cheese and stir until melted. Ladle into large bowls. Top with more Monterey Jack cheese and the sour cream, if desired.

Note: My son loves pepper Jack cheese. So if you're looking for a little extra zing in this dish, substitute shredded pepper Jack for some of the Monterey Jack.

Makes 8–10 servings

Baked Orange Roughy

This dish boasts a beautiful combination of colors and flavors. It comes together very quickly and needs only a simple salad to make your meal complete.

2 pounds orange roughy fillets

½ medium yellow onion, diced

2 ribs celery, diced

½ cup diced tomatoes

1 (14-ounce) can artichoke hearts, drained and quartered

2 tablespoons butter

¼ cup freshly squeezed lemon juice

1 bay leaf

¼ cup grated Parmesan cheese

Preheat the oven to 350°F.

Cut the fillets into serving-size pieces and place in a medium baking dish. In a medium skillet, sauté the onion, celery, tomatoes, and artichoke hearts in the butter over medium heat until the onion is soft, about 3 minutes. Add the lemon juice and bay leaf and cook for an additional 3 minutes. Pour the sauce over the fish. Cover and bake for 15 minutes. Uncover and continue baking for an additional 5 minutes. Discard the bay leaf and sprinkle with cheese before serving.

Makes 4 servings

Southwestern Egg Casserole

This is a twist on those overnight breakfast casseroles we have all tried. I have served it to a bunch of coaches and athletes and it is always a hit.

10 eggs

1 cup half-and-half

1 (12-ounce) container cottage cheese

Salt and freshly ground black pepper

2 (3½-ounce) packages corn tortilla strips

1 pound sausage, browned, drained, and crumbled

1 cup shredded Mexican cheese blend

1 tablespoon chopped fresh chives

2 cups salsa, for serving

Coat a 9 by 13-inch baking dish with nonstick cooking spray.

The night before you plan to serve this dish, whisk the eggs in a large bowl until well beaten. Add the half-and-half, cottage cheese, and salt and pepper. Blend well.

Place the tortilla strips in the bottom of the prepared baking dish. Scatter the cooked sausage evenly over the tortilla strips. Pour the egg mixture over all. Top with the Mexican cheese. Sprinkle the chives over the cheese. Cover with aluminum foil and refrigerate overnight.

In the morning, preheat the oven to 325°F.

Bake the casserole, covered, for 45 minutes. Uncover and bake for an additional 20 minutes, or until set. Let stand for 5 minutes before serving. Cut into squares. Pass the salsa.

Makes 12 servings

Wisdom Roast

I have to admit straight out that I have never been an expert on the preparation of meats. I set my mind on learning more in the past few years, though. I just keep asking questions and gathering advice from friends and family members. I have collected lists of "secrets" and all kinds of marinade concoctions.

It just seems right to present this roast recipe in this very unorthodox manner, since that is how it has come to me. With each step, I'll quote one of my experienced friends and you'll see how the collective wisdom of these ladies will richly reward you.

Step One: Choose the right type of beef roast. Chris Kleiber and Gayle Wheeler suggest one of these two cuts: chuck 7-bone roast or chuck-eye roast (primal cut: chuck/shoulder). Either one of these cuts, if prepared correctly, will be tender, juicy, and full of flavor.

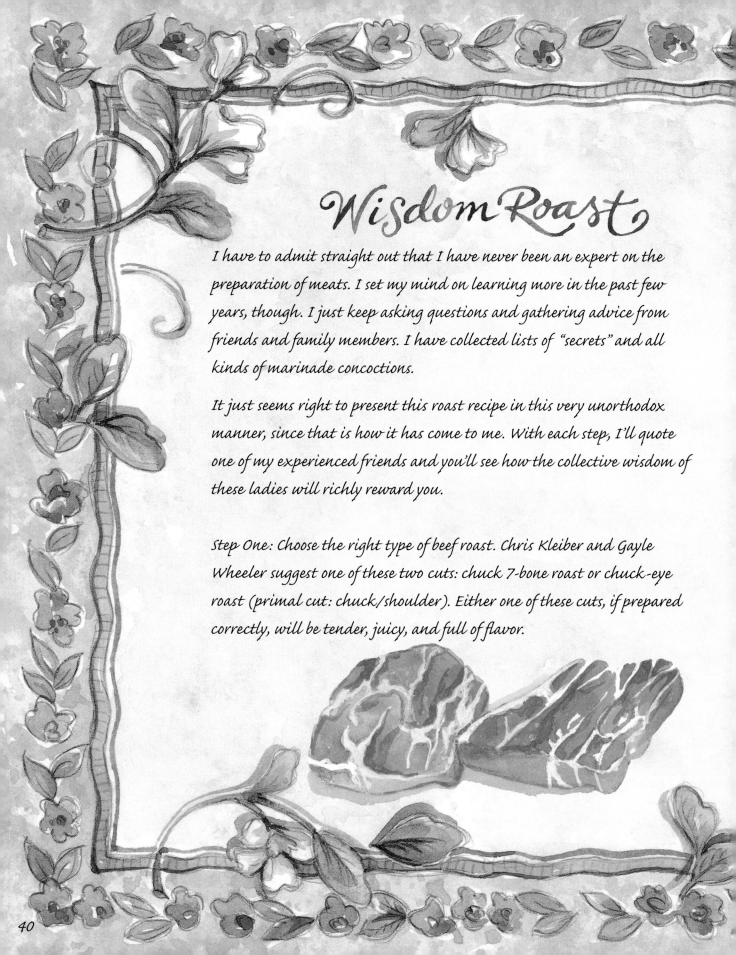

Step Two: Assemble a great collection of seasonings to prepare the roast. Diane Franklin suggests using these seasonings for the most basic roast beef dinner:

Montreal Steak Seasoning
Salt and freshly ground black pepper

Diane seasons the roast on both sides with these ingredients and then places it in a large zip-top plastic bag, squeezing out as much air as possible as she zips it shut. She then leaves it in the refrigerator for at least 3 hours (or overnight).

Step Three: Prepare the vegetables. This is a "duke's mixture," which includes just about anything I've ever seen served with a roast. You may omit the mushrooms if you like, but I highly recommend including everything else listed.

4 potatoes, peeled and sliced into 1-inch pieces
4 carrots, peeled and sliced into 1-inch pieces
1 medium yellow onion, coarsely chopped
1 rib celery, coarsely chopped
2 cloves garlic, minced
4 ounces white mushrooms, sliced

Step Four: Janet Baker says, "Sear that piece of meat on all sides to seal in the juices!" Heat 2 tablespoons of vegetable oil in a heavy skillet over medium-high until just smoking. Add the roast and brown well on all sides, turning with tongs (not a fork). Transfer the roast to a plate and set aside.

Step Five: Okay, this is my own personal bit of wisdom: Brown those veggies! Reserving the oil left in the pan after searing the beef, add all the vegetables listed and cook over medium heat until lightly browned (not tender, just browned). Remove from the heat.

Step Six: If I learned anything from Mrs. Chiles about cooking during the time I spent with the Chiles family when I was in high school, it was this: A little bit of sugar can make a big flavor difference. So, sprinkle about 2 teaspoons of sugar over the vegetables and cook for an additional 30 seconds.

Step Seven: This little secret I learned from my mom, Phyllis: canned French onion soup! Transfer the roast to a roasting pan. Surround it with the browned vegetables, including all those little "flavor bits" in the bottom of the pan. Then pour 1 (14-ounce) can of French onion soup over all. Cover with a lid or aluminum foil.

Step Eight: Slow and low. Actually that line came from a golf lesson I once had. But it also applies to a roast! Keep the oven temperature at 250°F–300°F and roast slowly until it reaches the desired doneness. This could take between 1½ to 3 hours, depending on the size of your roast. I suggest using a meat thermometer to determine doneness. Your thermometer should be labeled, but if not, here is a quick guide:

Rare: 140°F

Medium: 160°F

Medium-well: 170°F

Step Nine: Let it be. This advice comes from my friend Cathy Palmer. I'm sure when Cathy shares this advice with friends like me, it generally has absolutely nothing to do with roast. But, still it applies. Let the roast rest for about 10 minutes before slicing and serving.

Step Ten: A word about wisdom. At some time between the "slow and low" and the "let it be," make a list of your wisest friends, even if it's just a mental list. In times of trouble (and trust me, there will be trouble), you want those people within reach. Now thank God for them!

A special thank-you to <u>all</u> the wise women in my life.

The Sisters' Meat Loaf

This recipe is from Gail Hessenkemper, who shared it with her sister, who shared it with my sister, who shared it with me. Don't worry; there will not be a test on that information.

2 pounds lean ground beef
1 (3-ounce) envelope dry onion soup mix
⅔ cup milk
1 egg, beaten
1 cup dry bread crumbs

Sauce
⅓ cup firmly packed brown sugar
⅓ cup ketchup
2 tablespoons prepared mustard
1 teaspoon Worcestershire sauce

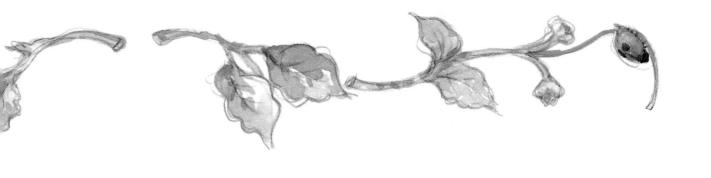

Preheat the oven to 350°F.

In a large bowl, combine the beef, soup mix, milk, egg, and bread crumbs. Mix with your hands until well blended. Transfer this mixture into a standard-size loaf pan. I use a ceramic baking dish shaped like a loaf pan for this recipe.

Prepare the sauce by combining the sugar, ketchup, mustard, and Worcestershire, whisking until well blended. Reserve half the sauce to serve tableside, and spread the other half on top of the meat.

Bake for 1 hour. Let stand for 5–10 minutes. Remove the extra fat from the sides of the pan by placing a folded paper towel along each edge. After soaking up the fat, discard the paper towel. Warm the reserved sauce and serve.

Makes 4–6 servings

Herzeghs' Swiss Chicken

This is such a pleasant chicken dish. It's not complicated or complex. It's just right when combined with some fresh vegetables and rice. Thank you to my friends Paul and Katherine Herzegh for sharing their time and their recipe with me.

4 boneless, skinless chicken breasts
4 slices swiss cheese
1 (10¾-ounce) can cream of chicken soup
½ cup white wine or chicken broth
½ cup crushed preseasoned croutons
¼ cup butter, melted

Preheat the oven to 350°F. Place the chicken in a large baking dish. Cover each piece of chicken with a slice of cheese.

Combine the soup with the wine and mix until blended. Spoon this mixture over the chicken and cheese. Scatter the crushed croutons evenly over the top. Drizzle the melted butter over all. Bake for 25–30 minutes.

Makes 4 servings

This is a pretty foolproof way to grill chicken breasts. I've found that it makes sense to grill an entire package of breasts at once, freezing what you won't need immediately to use for future meals. We eat a lot of chicken, and it's so nice to have sliced grilled chicken in the freezer to bring into a recipe on a moment's notice.

2½ pounds boneless, skinless chicken breasts
Salt and freshly ground black pepper

Preheat the grill to medium.

Spray each side of the chicken breasts with nonstick olive oil cooking spray. Season both sides with salt and pepper.

Using tongs, arrange the chicken on the grill, being careful not to crowd or overlap. Grill for 12–14 minutes. Turn with the tongs and grill the other side for an additional 12–14 minutes, or until the juices run clear when cut open at the thickest part of the breast. If using a meat thermometer, it should register 180°F when inserted into the thickest part. Transfer to a clean serving platter. Let rest for 5 minutes before serving or slicing.

Makes 6–8 servings

Dee's Sweet and Savory Wraps

This recipe is from my good friend Dee Stoelting. Those of you who have purchased our cookbooks before probably have enjoyed one or more of Dee's recipes from those books. My daughter would list these wraps as one of her top ten favorites, I think.

1 tablespoon vegetable oil

2 tablespoons soy sauce

4 teaspoons peanut butter

2 teaspoons hot sauce

2 teaspoons Montreal Steak Seasoning

2 boneless, skinless chicken breasts

2 tablespoons honey

2 tablespoons rice wine or cider vinegar

½ cucumber, seeded and sliced into julienne strips

4 large spinach tortillas

1 (6-ounce) jar sweet-and-sour (duck) sauce

½ teaspoon crushed red pepper flakes

8 slices provolone cheese

½ red bell pepper, thinly sliced

4 green onions, green part only, thinly sliced

1 cup loosely packed bean sprouts

¼ cup loosely packed chopped fresh cilantro

Preheat the oven to 350°F. Preheat the grill to medium.

Mix the vegetable oil, soy sauce, peanut butter, hot sauce, and steak seasoning together in a small bowl. Marinate the chicken in this mixture for 20–30 minutes. Discard the marinade. Then grill the chicken (see Grilled Chicken Breasts 101, page 47). Let the chicken rest for 10 minutes, then cut into thin slices.

In a small bowl, mix the honey and vinegar. Marinate the cucumber in this mixture for 15–20 minutes.

Generously spread each tortilla with the sweet-and-sour sauce. Sprinkle with a little of the red pepper flakes. Top with 2 slices of cheese, some chicken slices, and some bell pepper slices.

Transfer the tortillas to a baking sheet. Toast the tortillas in the oven for 5–7 minutes, until the cheese is bubbly. Remove from the oven and top with the onions, sprouts, and cilantro. Roll up each tortilla, tucking in the ends. Secure each wrap with two toothpicks and cut in half. Serve warm.

Makes 4 servings

RO-TEL Chicken

When I asked my friend Janice Manley to share a recipe for this book, she immediately thought of her friend Ritta Bailey and this dish. Jan says that Ritta is closer than a sister to her — a source of constant encouragement through the years as their husbands were stationed together in the Air Force in Colorado.

¾ cup butter

1 medium yellow onion, diced

1 cup chopped red bell pepper

1 (1-pound) package Velveeta cheese, cubed

1 (10-ounce) can RO-TEL tomatoes

¼ cup sour cream

4 boneless, skinless chicken breasts, cooked and thinly sliced

6 ounces penne pasta, cooked according to package directions and drained

1 cup frozen peas

36 butter-flavored crackers

Salt and freshly ground black pepper

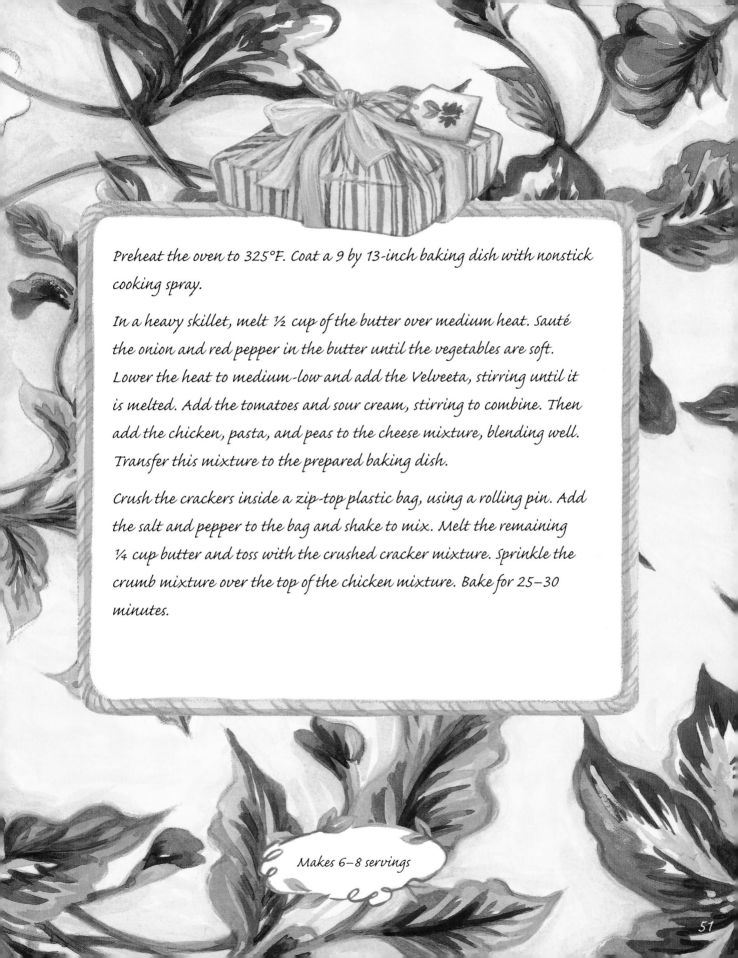

Preheat the oven to 325°F. Coat a 9 by 13-inch baking dish with nonstick cooking spray.

In a heavy skillet, melt ½ cup of the butter over medium heat. Sauté the onion and red pepper in the butter until the vegetables are soft. Lower the heat to medium-low and add the Velveeta, stirring until it is melted. Add the tomatoes and sour cream, stirring to combine. Then add the chicken, pasta, and peas to the cheese mixture, blending well. Transfer this mixture to the prepared baking dish.

Crush the crackers inside a zip-top plastic bag, using a rolling pin. Add the salt and pepper to the bag and shake to mix. Melt the remaining ¼ cup butter and toss with the crushed cracker mixture. Sprinkle the crumb mixture over the top of the chicken mixture. Bake for 25–30 minutes.

Makes 6–8 servings

The Baker Girls' Pizza Turnovers

Whitney, Blaire, and Haley Baker share this fun recipe — it can also be prepared as an appetizer by cutting the pizza dough into smaller pieces. We love it both ways.

1 tablespoon olive oil

8 ounces Italian sausage

1 cup tightly packed fresh spinach cut into strips

4 ounces cream cheese, softened

⅓ cup grated Parmesan cheese, plus ¼ cup

½ teaspoon salt

¼ teaspoon freshly ground black pepper

1 (13½-ounce) package refrigerated pizza dough

Flour, for rolling out the dough

1 egg, beaten

1½ cups marinara sauce, for dipping

Whitney

Preheat the oven to 400°F. Coat a large baking sheet with nonstick cooking spray.

Heat the olive oil over medium-high heat in a heavy skillet. Add sausage and cook until crumbled and golden brown, about 5 minutes. Add the spinach and cook until wilted. Turn off the heat and let cool for about 10 minutes. Add the cream cheese, ⅓ cup of the Parmesan, the salt and pepper. Stir to combine. Set aside.

Roll out the pizza dough on a lightly floured surface to a thin 12 by 20-inch rectangle. Cut the rectangle in half lengthwise. Then cut each half into 4 equal rectangles.

Place a few heaping tablespoons of the sausage and cheese mixture on one side of each rectangle. Using a pastry brush, brush the edges of the rectangles with the beaten egg. Close the rectangles of pizza dough over the filling and seal with the tines of a fork. Place the pizza pockets onto the prepared baking sheet. Brush the top of each pocket with the beaten egg. Sprinkle with the remaining ¼ cup of the cheese.

Bake until golden brown, 12–15 minutes.

Heat the marinara sauce over low heat in a medium saucepan. Serve the hot pockets with the marinara sauce for dipping.

Makes 4–6 servings

Pork Tenderloin with Ginger Glaze

This is another tasty recipe from our good friends the Bakers. I love the aroma that fills the kitchen when the tenderloin is in the oven. I was surprised how quickly the recipe came together the first time I made it. Try it with Sweet Ginger Carrots (page 69) and Macadamia Wild Rice Pilaf (page 74).

2 pounds pork tenderloin

½ teaspoon sea salt

⅓ cup apricot preserves

3 cloves garlic, minced

1 tablespoon water

1 tablespoon soy sauce

1 teaspoon ground ginger

Green onion strips, for garnish

Preheat the oven to 425°F.

Place the pork tenderloin on a lightly greased rack in an aluminum foil–lined roasting pan. Sprinkle evenly with the salt.

Combine the preserves, garlic, water, soy sauce, and ginger in a small bowl and mix well. Spread this mixture evenly over the pork.

Bake for 25 minutes or until a meat thermometer inserted at the thickest point registers 155°F. Remove from the oven. Cover and let stand for 10 minutes. Garnish with green onion strips.

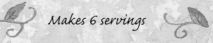 Makes 6 servings

Kinderhook Quiche

My friend Jayne Wake loves this crustless quiche recipe because it's so quick and easy. It allows more time for fun while they are at their lake home. I found it's also a great way to use leftover meats or vegetables.

4 to 5 eggs

½ cup butter, melted

1½ cups milk

⅔ cup biscuit mix

¼ teaspoon salt

¼ teaspoon freshly ground black pepper

1 cup shredded Cheddar cheese

¾ cup cooked ham (or sausage, bacon, crab, or shrimp)

Preheat the oven to 350°F.

Combine the eggs, butter, milk, biscuit mix, salt, and pepper in a blender or mixer bowl. Blend until smooth. Pour this mixture into a 9-inch pie pan or quiche dish. Add the cheese and ham, pushing them below the surface of the liquid. Bake for 45 minutes, or until set.

Makes 6–8 servings

Zippy Omelets

Jennifer Weaver is not only my friend but she is also the nurse who stood by me through the birth and delivery of my daughter, Brooke. When it comes to newborns, Jennifer is your girl! It goes without saying that I have put a lot of trust in her through the years. So, when she first told me about this recipe, I thought it sounded really interesting and believed it could work. But I didn't anticipate 1) how positively yummy these omelets would be, and 2) how a recipe like this can turn an ordinary breakfast into a fun-filled way to start your day! Thank you, Jennifer!

This is such a great way to feed a bunch of people quickly. What I love about this is the fact that each person is actually creating his or her own omelet "to order." The lion's share of the work is done the night before, leaving you free from most of the cleanup the following morning. This is how it works:

Step One: Fill a basket with enough zip-top plastic freezer bags to accommodate each guest. Fill a large bowl with enough eggs to allow 2 eggs per guest. Prepare a little buffet of ingredients that might be good choices for filling an omelet. Here are some possibilities:

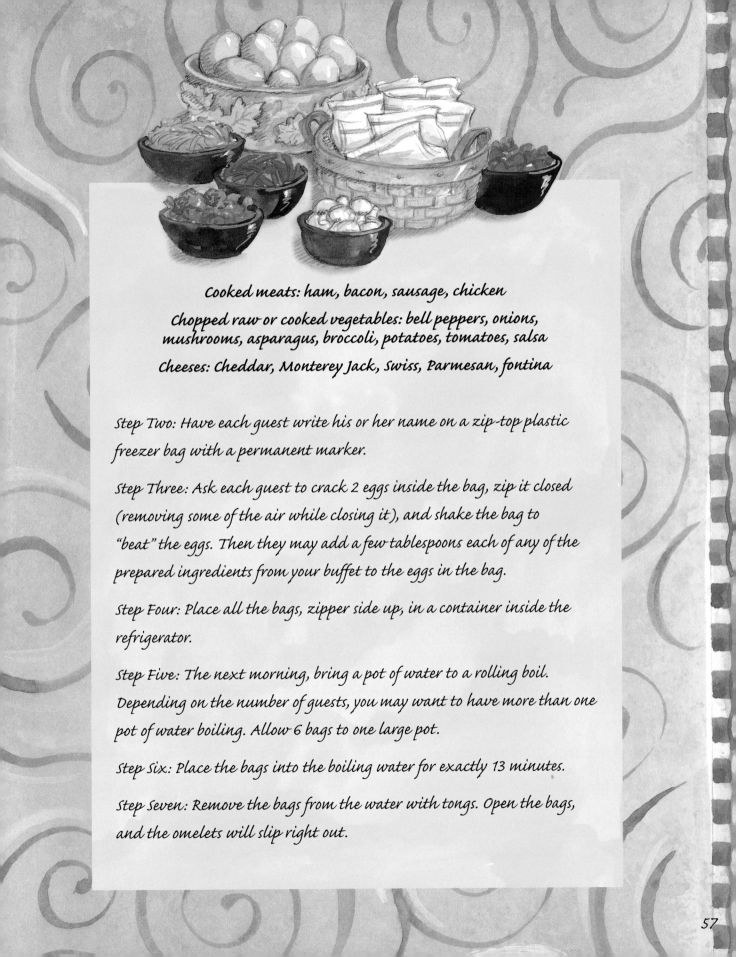

Cooked meats: ham, bacon, sausage, chicken

Chopped raw or cooked vegetables: bell peppers, onions, mushrooms, asparagus, broccoli, potatoes, tomatoes, salsa

Cheeses: Cheddar, Monterey Jack, Swiss, Parmesan, fontina

Step Two: Have each guest write his or her name on a zip-top plastic freezer bag with a permanent marker.

Step Three: Ask each guest to crack 2 eggs inside the bag, zip it closed (removing some of the air while closing it), and shake the bag to "beat" the eggs. Then they may add a few tablespoons each of any of the prepared ingredients from your buffet to the eggs in the bag.

Step Four: Place all the bags, zipper side up, in a container inside the refrigerator.

Step Five: The next morning, bring a pot of water to a rolling boil. Depending on the number of guests, you may want to have more than one pot of water boiling. Allow 6 bags to one large pot.

Step Six: Place the bags into the boiling water for exactly 13 minutes.

Step Seven: Remove the bags from the water with tongs. Open the bags, and the omelets will slip right out.

Spinach & Chicken Pasta Bake

Soon after the decision was made to write another cookbook, my daughter, Brooke, and I began experimenting with this dish. After the first bite, we exchanged that wide-eyed-head-nodding-that's-what-I'm-talkin'-about look. This recipe was a keeper, we agreed. We think you'll love it, too.

1 tablespoon olive oil

⅔ cup chopped yellow onion

1 (10-ounce) package frozen chopped spinach, thawed

8 ounces rigatoni, cooked according to package directions and drained

3 cups cubed cooked chicken

1 (14½-ounce) can diced tomatoes

1 (8-ounce) package cream cheese, softened

1 teaspoon salt

½ teaspoon freshly ground black pepper

1½ cups shredded mozzarella cheese

Preheat the oven to 375°F. Coat the bottom of a 7 by 11-inch baking dish with the olive oil.

Add the onion to the baking dish in a single layer. Bake for 15 minutes, until the onion is tender. Transfer to a large bowl and set aside.

Drain the spinach well, pressing out the moisture between paper towels. Combine the spinach, pasta, chicken, tomatoes, cream cheese, salt, and pepper with the onion in the bowl. Transfer to the baking dish and sprinkle with the mozzarella cheese. Bake, covered, for 30 minutes. Uncover and bake for an additional 15 minutes. Serve warm.

Makes 6–8 servings

Party Pizza Dough

Just in case you don't have a recipe for pizza dough, here is a quick and easy one to use. The great thing about using this recipe is it makes enough dough for each guest to have a personal pizza. Speaking of that, use this recipe for the Personal Pizzas on the Grill (page 62). The dough can be refrigerated for up to 3 days or frozen for up to 3 months.

5 cups all-purpose flour, plus up to 1 cup for kneading

1 tablespoon sugar

2 teaspoons salt

1 teaspoon quick-rise yeast (about ½ of one of those ¼-ounce packets if you are not using a jar of yeast)

3 ½ tablespoons olive oil

1¾ cups water, at room temperature

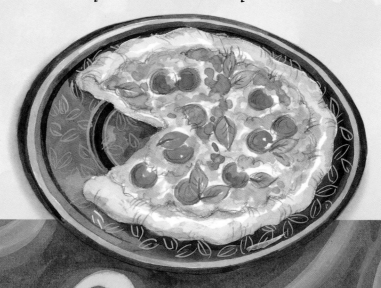

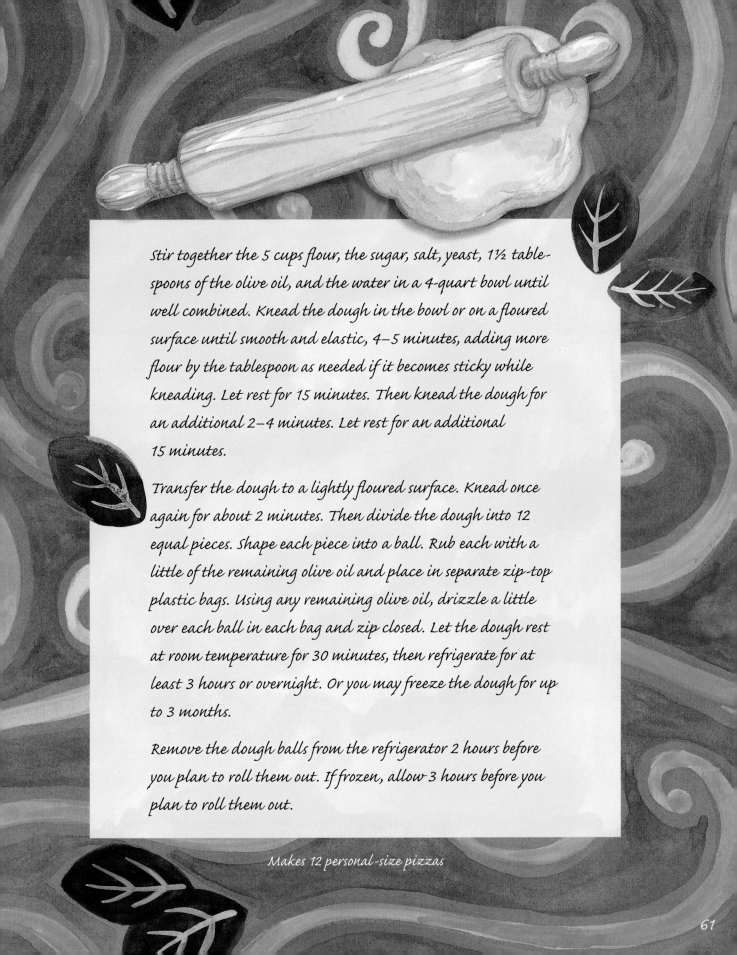

Stir together the 5 cups flour, the sugar, salt, yeast, 1½ table-spoons of the olive oil, and the water in a 4-quart bowl until well combined. Knead the dough in the bowl or on a floured surface until smooth and elastic, 4–5 minutes, adding more flour by the tablespoon as needed if it becomes sticky while kneading. Let rest for 15 minutes. Then knead the dough for an additional 2–4 minutes. Let rest for an additional 15 minutes.

Transfer the dough to a lightly floured surface. Knead once again for about 2 minutes. Then divide the dough into 12 equal pieces. Shape each piece into a ball. Rub each with a little of the remaining olive oil and place in separate zip-top plastic bags. Using any remaining olive oil, drizzle a little over each ball in each bag and zip closed. Let the dough rest at room temperature for 30 minutes, then refrigerate for at least 3 hours or overnight. Or you may freeze the dough for up to 3 months.

Remove the dough balls from the refrigerator 2 hours before you plan to roll them out. If frozen, allow 3 hours before you plan to roll them out.

Makes 12 personal-size pizzas

Personal Pizzas on the Grill

There is a wonderful recipe for pizza dough (Party Pizza Dough, page 60) in this book. But you may certainly use another recipe or a refrigerated pizza dough of your choice to create these little pizzas. Depending on the size of your gathering, you may need more or less of the ingredients listed as toppings.

Pizza dough (page 60), divided into 4–6 pieces

Olive oil, for brushing

1 (26-ounce) jar marinara or pizza sauce

4 cups shredded mozzarella cheese

1 pound sausage and/or pepperoni, chicken, or Canadian bacon (cooked if raw)

Assorted vegetable toppings of your choice to equal about 3 cups

Preheat the grill to medium-low.

Roll out a piece of the pizza dough and transfer to a large baking sheet. Brush or spray lightly with olive oil. (You may be able to prepare more than one pizza at a time, depending on the size of your grill.)

Place the dough, oil side down, on the grill and cook for 4–5 minutes, until lightly browned on the bottom. Transfer the dough back to the baking sheet, grilled side up. Top with the ingredients listed and then return to the grill. Cook until the cheese melts and the dough has a chance to brown lightly on the bottom, 4–5 minutes. Repeat as needed until all the pizzas are grilled. It is helpful if you use a large metal spatula when transferring the pizzas from the grill to the baking sheet, and then onto serving plates.

Makes 4–6 servings

Chicken-Chile Quiche

This is a very hearty quiche with a nice zippy flavor. Serve with a little salad topped with some avocado slices to make the meal complete.

1 unbaked 9-inch pastry shell

1½ cups sliced grilled chicken breast

½ cup shredded Monterey Jack cheese

½ cup shredded Colby cheese

½ cup chopped green chiles

¼ cup chopped green onion

3 eggs, beaten

½ cup mayonnaise

¾ cup milk

½ teaspoon dried oregano

Salt and freshly ground black pepper

2 cloves garlic, minced

Preheat the oven to 375°F. Pierce the pastry shell all over with a fork. Bake for 10 minutes.

Lower the oven temperature to 350°F. Combine the chicken, cheeses, chiles, and onion in a large bowl until well mixed. Transfer this mixture to the pastry shell.

Stir together the eggs, mayonnaise, milk, oregano, salt and pepper, and garlic, blending until smooth. Pour over the chicken mixture. Bake for 40 minutes or until a knife inserted in the center comes out clean.

Makes 6–8 servings

Invisible Guests

As I was writing this book, it became clear to me that "living ideals" are at our table in addition to our food, family, and friends. These invisible guests each represent something that enhances our mealtime together:

- Restoration: We restore our strength —physically and emotionally— during this time.

- Nature: Gathering together for meals gives us an opportunity to recognize our relationship with nature.

- Past and Present Joy: We enjoy those who are present around our table and remember those who are absent from us.

- The Artist: The table is a blank canvas for those who approach meal preparation and table setting as their creative craft; it becomes an artistic expression of love.

  - Workshop Facilitator: We enjoy the advantages of sharing ideas and learning from others.

  - Thrive and Survive Guide: We celebrate the highlights of our day, face to face, and receive encouragement to deal with our disappointments.

Side Dishes and Salads

Sweet Green Beans

There just isn't a better way to describe these green beans. My friend Kelly Garr brought these to our annual Easter dinner at her parents' house a few years ago. Now this dish is as much a part of our Easter festivities as the Wiffle ball tournament on the front lawn.

8 slices bacon

2 (14½-ounce) cans whole green beans

½ cup butter

¾ cup firmly packed brown sugar

2 teaspoons garlic powder

Salt

Preheat the oven to 350°F.

Cook the bacon in a skillet until almost done, but not crisp. Drain the fat from the bacon by placing it on paper towels. When cool enough to handle, cut each piece in half crosswise and wrap around a bundle of 8 or 9 green beans. Secure with a toothpick. Repeat until all the green beans are bundled.

Place the bundles in a medium baking dish. Melt the butter in a heavy saucepan and add the brown sugar, garlic powder, and salt. Stir until it begins to boil. Remove the butter mixture from the heat and pour evenly over the top of the beans. Bake for 20 minutes.

Serves 6–8

Broccoli Salad

We all know how good broccoli is for us. It is categorized as one of the "super foods," so it's wise to have at least a half a dozen recipes in your cooking repertoire featuring it as the star that it is. Here is one of ours.

4 cups chopped broccoli

½ cup dried cranberries

¼ cup chopped red onion

2 tablespoons sugar

3 tablespoons white vinegar

1 cup mayonnaise (I use a light version)

½ teaspoon salt

½ teaspoon freshly ground black pepper

10 slices bacon, cooked crisp and crumbled

1 cup sunflower seeds or chopped almonds, toasted (page 147)

In a large bowl, combine the broccoli, cranberries, and onion. In a small bowl, whisk together the sugar, vinegar, and mayonnaise. Pour the dressing over the broccoli mixture and toss to coat. Season with the salt and pepper. Cover and refrigerate. Just before serving, add the bacon and sunflower seeds. Toss to combine.

Serves 6–8

Grape Salad

Thank you to Susan Brown and Wanda Knight for sharing this recipe. This is a really tasty alternative as a side dish with sandwiches in place of chips or a garden salad.

¼ cup sour cream

4 ounces cream cheese, softened

¼ cup granulated sugar

½ teaspoon vanilla extract

1 pound seedless red grapes

1 pound seedless green grapes

½ cup brown sugar

½ cup chopped pecans

In a medium bowl, combine the sour cream, cream cheese, granulated sugar, and vanilla. Mix with a whisk until smooth. Add the grapes and gently mix. Sprinkle the brown sugar over the top and finish with the chopped pecans.

Note: My family found this salad to be sweet enough without the addition of the brown sugar on top. You might try adjusting the sugar amounts to fit your personal tastes.

Serves 6

Jayne's Strawberry-Mandarin Tossed Salad

When I think of this salad, I picture sitting around Jim and Jayne Wake's table in Old Kinderhook, enjoying their company along with all of Jayne's good cooking. Those are precious moments for me, just reflecting on how God has blessed my family with such openhearted friends.

You will love this salad — it is full of flavor and blended textures, but is also light and refreshing!

Dressing

¼ cup sugar

2 tablespoons honey

½ teaspoon paprika

½ teaspoon minced onion

2 tablespoons apple cider vinegar

1¼ teaspoons freshly squeezed lemon juice

½ teaspoon dry mustard

¼ teaspoon celery seed

Salad

8 cups mixed salad greens

2 cups strawberries, stemmed and sliced

1 (11-ounce) can mandarin oranges, drained

1 red onion, sliced

⅓ cup slivered almonds, toasted (page 147)

4 slices bacon, cooked crisp and crumbled

In a small bowl, combine all the dressing ingredients. Whisk together until well blended.

In a large bowl, combine all the salad ingredients, tossing to mix. Chill until ready to serve. Just before serving, add the dressing and toss again.

Serves 6–8

Mrs. Chiles's Glazed Fruit Salad

This recipe is from my second mom, Mrs. Chiles. Many of you who have purchased our other books will remember this precious lady as the one responsible for converting me into a vegetable lover when I was a teenager. She is an amazing cook, and I'm happy to share her very simple but refreshing fruit salad recipe.

1 (21-ounce) can pineapple chunks in juice
1 (21-ounce) can fruit cocktail in juice
2 (11-ounce) cans mandarin oranges in juice
1 (21-ounce) can peach pie filling
6 or 7 bananas, sliced

Drain the juice from the pineapple chunks, fruit cocktail, and mandarin oranges. Combine the fruit with the peach pie filling in a large glass serving bowl. Cover and chill for several hours or overnight. Fold in the bananas just before serving.

Serves 12

Penne Pasta Salad

I know you'll enjoy this nice, light pasta salad. This is another good choice for when it's more convenient to prepare a dish the day before you need it.

1 (1-pound) package penne pasta, cooked according to package directions and drained

1 cup white or balsamic vinegar

1 cup sugar

2 teaspoons salt

1 teaspoon freshly ground black pepper

1 small onion, chopped

2 medium cucumbers, thinly sliced

1 medium tomato, seeded and chopped

1 red or green bell pepper, chopped

1 teaspoon Dijon mustard

½ teaspoon celery seed

½ cup olive oil

Mix all the ingredients in a large bowl (be sure to do it in the order listed). Toss until well mixed. Cover and refrigerate overnight before serving.

Serves 8–10

Ellen's Holiday Berry Salad

My stepmom, Donna, usually brings this dish to my sister's home for Thanksgiving if she and my dad are in town. She got the recipe from her friend Ellen. Thanks to both of them for sharing! I like it because the tartness of the cranberries is balanced with the sweetness of the strawberries.

1 (10-ounce) package frozen strawberries in syrup
1 (12-ounce) package fresh or frozen cranberries
½ cup sugar

Drain the frozen strawberries, reserving the syrup. Add enough water to the syrup to make 1 cup of liquid. Combine the syrup mixture with the cranberries and sugar in a heavy saucepan. Bring the mixture to a boil and cook, stirring occasionally, until the cranberries split open. Remove from the heat and add the strawberries. Transfer to a serving dish and cover. Chill for 3 hours before serving.

Serves 6–8

Mac and Cheese

This is a classic. Just in case you've never experienced the kind of macaroni and cheese that doesn't come from a can or a box, please try this sometime when you've got 30 or 40 minutes to play in the kitchen. You won't regret it, I promise, and you'll never go back to the box.

8 ounces elbow or shell macaroni

2 tablespoons butter

2 tablespoons all-purpose flour

2 cups milk

1 teaspoon salt

½ teaspoon freshly ground black pepper

¼ teaspoon ground red pepper

2 cups shredded Cheddar cheese

Preheat the oven to 400°F. Coat a 2-quart baking dish with nonstick cooking spray.

Prepare the pasta according to the package directions.

While the pasta is cooking, melt the butter in a large saucepan. Add the flour and stir constantly with a whisk for 2 minutes. Gradually add the milk, stirring constantly for 7–8 minutes or until thickened. Remove from the heat and stir in the salt, black and red peppers, and 1 cup of the cheese.

Drain the pasta, fold it into the sauce, and transfer the mixture to the prepared baking dish. Top with the remaining 1 cup cheese and bake for 20 minutes or until bubbly.

Serves 4–6

I'll Have What She's Having

When I am reminded of all I've been taught by different women in my lifetime, I am just overwhelmed by my good fortune. If I allowed myself to reminisce about these ladies, I could quickly relate to you how each one of them brought something unique and beautiful into my life.

From one, I learned to sew. Another taught me how to learn to love vegetables (and as a bonus, how to learn to love myself). From my mom, I learned about independence. From my sister, I learned how to receive encouragement.

Not too long ago, my daughter gave me a beautiful handwritten note. In the note she explained that she had been studying certain virtues, and that those virtues reminded her of me. She wanted to thank me for what that meant to her. There are no words to express how moved I was by her sentiment. To think that I could give as I had received brought me so much joy.

Whether we feel we deserve this kind of admiration or not, there is a very good chance that there is a person out there in the world who wants to be just like you or just like me. If they're having what we're having, would you be so kind as to pass me the salt of the earth?

Gal 5:22-23

"But the fruit of the Spirit is love, joy, peace, longsuffering, gentleness, goodness, faith, meekness, temperance: against such there is no law."

Breads, Muffins & Spreads

The Creed's Sleepover Breakfast Bread

My friend Abi Krulatz has such sweet memories of her father preparing this treat whenever she had overnight guests. Abi says the tradition started when she was in grade school and will continue on with her now that she has children of her own. This recipe is proof that a few moments well invested can make memories that last several lifetimes!

2 tablespoons butter or shortening (Abi's dad uses Crisco)
1 loaf frozen bread dough
1 cup sugar
1½ cups heavy whipping cream
4 teaspoons ground cinnamon

Before bedtime, coat a 9 by 13-inch baking dish with nonstick cooking spray. Rub the butter over the surface of the frozen bread dough and place in the baking dish. Cover the dish with plastic wrap and allow the dough to thaw and rise overnight at room temperature.

In the morning, preheat the oven to 375°F. Stretch the dough out to fit the baking dish, and poke holes in the dough with your fingertips.

Sprinkle the sugar evenly over the surface of the dough. Pour the cream over the top. Sprinkle with the cinnamon. Bake for 28–30 minutes. Serve warm.

Serves 4–6

Beehive Butter

This is such a simple thing. But, like so many other simple things in our lives (a kiss, a hug, a sincere compliment), it can make all the difference! My family enjoys this butter with biscuits, dinner rolls, and corn bread.

2 teaspoons honey
½ cup butter, softened
1 pecan half (optional)

In a small dish, blend the honey into the butter with a fork until smooth and creamy.

If you want a more decorative look, transfer the butter to a small plate and shape into a "beehive." Scrape the outside of the mound of butter with a fork horizontally to resemble a hive. Place a pecan half at the bottom of the hive to resemble a "door." Chill slightly to maintain the shape of the mold.

Makes a generous ½ cup

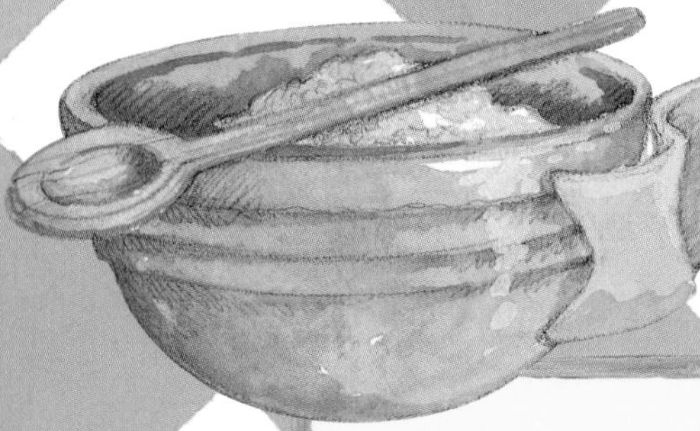

Honey Whole Wheat Bread

If you're looking for a healthy choice for sandwich bread or toast, this might be the recipe for you. Using quick-rise yeast will shorten the preparation time.

2 (¼-ounce) packages quick-rise yeast

2½ cups warm water

¼ cup honey

1 tablespoon sea salt

¼ cup butter, melted

7 cups whole wheat flour

In a mixer bowl, dissolve the yeast in the warm water. Stir in the honey, salt, and butter. Add the flour, 1 cup at a time, to the yeast mixture, mixing well after each addition, until 6 of the 7 cups have been added. Cover the dough and let it rest for 10 minutes.

Continue by kneading the dough until smooth, elastic, and no longer tacky (6–8 minutes). You may add up to 1 cup of additional flour as you knead the dough. Place the dough in a greased bowl and turn once to coat. Cover with plastic wrap and let rise until doubled in size, about 45 minutes.

Preheat the oven to 350°F. Coat two 5 by 9-inch loaf pans with nonstick cooking spray.

Punch down the dough. Scatter a little wheat flour onto a clean work surface. Turn the dough out onto this floured surface. Divide the dough in half and shape into 2 loaves. Place the loaves into the prepared pans. Cover lightly with plastic wrap. Let the dough rise until it reaches the tops of the pans, 30–45 minutes.

Bake for 40–45 minutes, or until golden brown. Cool on a wire rack.

Makes 2 loaves

Peaches and Cream Muffins

My daughter, Brooke, made these muffins to serve at church. They were a big hit. We have also found that we can substitute other in-season fruits for the peaches. So feel free to experiment.

2 cups all-purpose flour

1 cup sugar

1½ teaspoons baking powder

½ teaspoon baking soda

6 tablespoons butter, cut up

1 cup buttermilk

3 tablespoons freshly squeezed orange juice

1 tablespoon grated orange peel

1 egg

1 cup peeled and chopped peaches

4 ounces cream cheese, cut into 12 cubes

Streusel Topping

⅓ cup all-purpose flour

3 tablespoons sugar

1 tablespoon freshly squeezed orange juice

2 tablespoons butter, softened

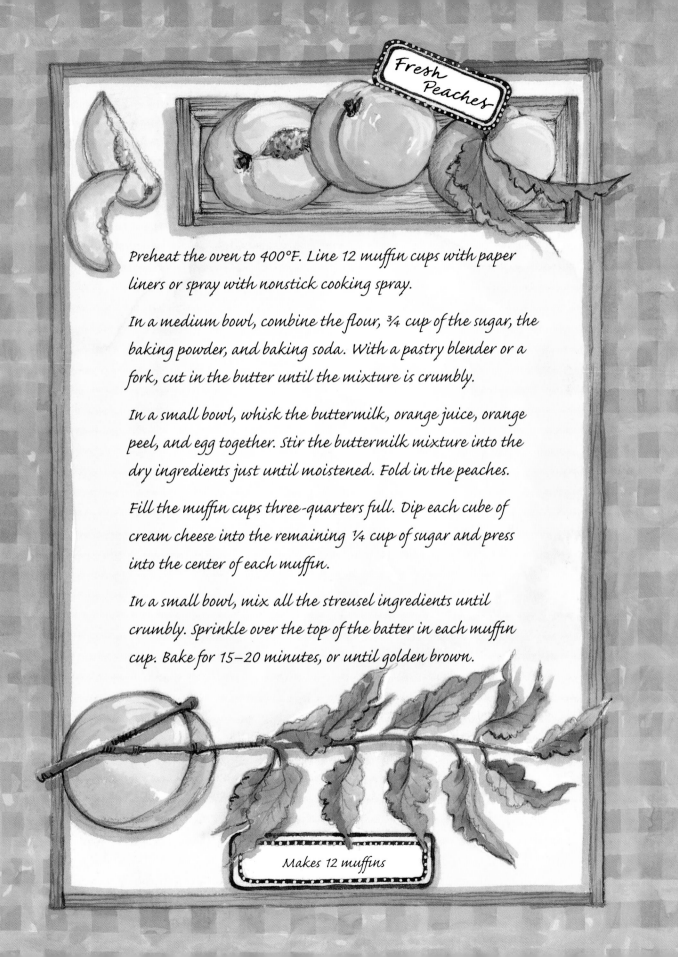

Fresh Peaches

Preheat the oven to 400°F. Line 12 muffin cups with paper liners or spray with nonstick cooking spray.

In a medium bowl, combine the flour, ¾ cup of the sugar, the baking powder, and baking soda. With a pastry blender or a fork, cut in the butter until the mixture is crumbly.

In a small bowl, whisk the buttermilk, orange juice, orange peel, and egg together. Stir the buttermilk mixture into the dry ingredients just until moistened. Fold in the peaches.

Fill the muffin cups three-quarters full. Dip each cube of cream cheese into the remaining ¼ cup of sugar and press into the center of each muffin.

In a small bowl, mix all the streusel ingredients until crumbly. Sprinkle over the top of the batter in each muffin cup. Bake for 15–20 minutes, or until golden brown.

Makes 12 muffins

Monkey Bread

This recipe is one of my daughter's favorites. She first enjoyed it at the Bakers' house after a sleepover. Is there anything that smells better than cinnamon, sugar, and butter bubbling in the oven?

3 (8-ounce) cans refrigerated biscuit dough
½ cup granulated sugar
1 teaspoon ground cinnamon
1 cup firmly packed brown sugar
½ cup butter, melted

Preheat the oven to 350°F. Coat a Bundt pan with nonstick cooking spray.

Cut each of the biscuits into quarters. Combine the sugar and cinnamon in a large zip-top plastic bag. Drop a dozen pieces of biscuit dough into the bag at one time. Shake until covered. Place in the Bundt pan, and repeat until all the biscuit pieces have been placed in the pan.

Combine the brown sugar with the melted butter. Mix well and pour over the top of all the biscuits.

Bake for 30–40 minutes, until golden brown. Cool slightly before turning over onto a serving platter.

Serves 8–10

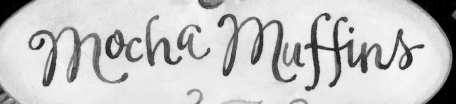

Mocha Muffins

This muffin recipe is a close cousin to the Sour Cream Muffins on page 96. To create this fun flavor, rather than adding a fruit or chocolate chip, use this mocha filling in the center of each muffin and finish with the Streusel Topping (page 97) right before baking.

Mocha Muffin Filling
4½ teaspoons instant espresso powder

4½ teaspoons cocoa

3 tablespoons sugar

Mix all the ingredients in a small bowl. When filling muffin cups, fill each halfway with batter, then a generous teaspoon of filling, an additional heaping tablespoon of batter, and, finally, the Streusel Topping. Bake according to the Sour Cream Muffin instructions.

Makes 24 muffins

Focaccia Bread

Ever since we purchased a panini grill to use at home, we've had so much fun inventing new sandwiches. Of course, experimenting with new sandwiches sometimes leads you to experimenting with new bread recipes. Even if you don't picture yourself as an expert bread baker, this is nearly foolproof.

1¼ cups mashed potatoes

½ cup milk

2 to 3 cups bread flour

1 tablespoon sea salt

½ cup olive oil

2 (¼-ounce) packages quick-rise yeast

1 cup grated Asiago cheese

Olive oil, for drizzling

½ cup chopped red onion

Sieve

Grease a 12 by 14-inch baking pan.

In a saucepan, warm the potatoes and milk to 120°F. Transfer to a mixer bowl. Add 1 cup of the flour, the salt, olive oil, and yeast. Mix on low speed for 1 minute. Add ½ cup of the flour and ½ cup of the cheese. Mix on low speed for 5–6 minutes, or by hand for 8–10 minutes, adding the remaining flour, 1 tablespoon at a time, as needed, to keep the dough from becoming too sticky. Oil the top of the dough and turn once. Cover and let rise until doubled in size, 35–40 minutes.

Roll out the dough on a floured surface until nearly the size of the prepared pan. Transfer the dough to the pan and stretch the dough to fit. With wet fingers, press your fingertips into the dough over the entire surface to create little valleys. Drizzle with the olive oil and sprinkle with the onion and the remaining ½ cup of cheese. Let rise until doubled, 15–20 minutes.

While the dough is rising, preheat the oven to 400°F.

Bake for 14–16 minutes, or until golden brown.

Serves 6–8

Sour Cream Muffins

This is another "Dee" recipe. That is pretty much all you'd have to say in our community and almost everyone would know to whom you were referring. Dee Stoelting has contributed a recipe to nearly every cookbook Shelly and I have ever done together. You will love this versatile recipe. Dee sometimes divides the batter and creates several different kinds of muffins with this one batch, using some of the options listed below.

1 cup butter, softened

1½ cups sugar

3 eggs

1 teaspoon vanilla extract

3 cups all-purpose flour

2½ teaspoons baking powder

1 teaspoon salt

¼ teaspoon baking soda

1 cup sour cream

½ cup milk

Add-ins — Choose any one of the following to fold into the batter:

1 cup blueberries

1 cup chocolate chips

⅓ cup each white chocolate chips, dried cranberries, and sliced almonds

Mocha Muffin Filling (page 93)

Streusel Topping*

1 cup sugar

½ cup all-purpose flour

½ cup butter, cold

_*As an alternative to the Streusel Topping, you may substitute
¼ cup of coarse sugar (also called sugar crystals)._

Preheat the oven to 350°F. Line 24 muffin cups with paper liners or coat with nonstick cooking spray.

In a mixer bowl, combine the butter and sugar, and beat until light and fluffy, about 2 minutes. Add the eggs, one at a time, beating well after each addition. Add the vanilla and blend well. Mix the flour, baking powder, salt, and baking soda together in a separate bowl. Blend the sour cream with the milk in a small bowl. Add the flour mixture to the sugar mixture alternately with the milk mixture, beginning and ending with the flour mixture. Fold in the add-in of your choice.

To prepare the Streusel Topping, mix all the ingredients together until crumbly. If it becomes sticky, put the mixture in the refrigerator until it chills. Then break up into crumbles. Top each muffin with the streusel mixture. Bake for 24–28 minutes, until a tester inserted into the middle of a muffin comes out clean.

Makes 24 muffins

Carol's Tasty Italian Biscuit Bites

Some of you may remember Carol Zimmer (a friend of my sister's), who shared one of her favorite recipes in one of our other books. When she heard we were doing another book, she e-mailed me a few more of her family's favorites. This one is so easy and is a great alternative to garlic bread. I also like the presentation of this — you'll see — it's fun! Thanks again, Carol!

½ cup butter, melted

2 teaspoons Italian seasoning

¼ teaspoon garlic powder

¼ teaspoon onion powder

¼ teaspoon freshly ground black pepper

12 frozen biscuits, cut into quarters

Preheat the oven to 425°F.

Mix the melted butter with the spices. Dip each piece of biscuit in this mixture and arrange side by side on a baking sheet. Bake for 8–10 minutes, or until golden brown.

Serves 6–8

Beer Batter Bread

I have some other beer bread recipes in my file from experimenting through the years, but this has become my new favorite. I think the blend of bread flour and wheat flour and the use of brown sugar give this bread an extra-rich flavor and really wonderful texture. It smells so heavenly in the oven that the whole family will want to hang out in the kitchen while it's baking!

2 cups bread flour

1 cup whole wheat flour

¼ cup brown sugar

1 tablespoon baking powder

1 teaspoon sea salt

1 (12-ounce) bottle or can of beer, unopened and at room temperature

½ cup butter, melted

Preheat the oven to 375°F. Coat a 5 by 9-inch loaf pan with nonstick cooking spray or butter.

In a medium bowl, stir together the flours, brown sugar, baking powder, and salt. Open the beer and add it all at once. Stir just until combined, about 25 strokes. The batter will be slightly lumpy. Pour the batter into the prepared pan and drizzle with the melted butter.

Bake until the top is crusty and a cake tester inserted in the center comes out clean, 35–40 minutes. Cool on a wire rack for 5 minutes before turning out of the pan. Serve warm or at room temperature.

Makes 1 loaf

Heirloom Rolls

You'll want to pass this recipe down to all generations that come after you. The first time I experimented with it, I could tell by the feel of the dough that the rolls would be wonderful—and they were! I enjoy the texture and taste of these rolls so much that I use the dough as a "foundation" for other types of rolls as well. See the Cinnamon Rolls recipe on page 102.

¾ cup buttermilk, warm

6 tablespoons butter, melted and slightly cooled

3 eggs, lightly beaten

4 cups all-purpose flour, plus more for kneading

¼ cup sugar

1 (¼-ounce) package quick-rise yeast

1½ teaspoons salt

Coat a baking sheet with nonstick cooking spray.

Whisk the buttermilk, butter, and eggs together in a large liquid measuring cup. Mix 4 cups of the flour, the sugar, yeast, and salt in a mixer bowl fitted with a dough hook. With the mixer on low speed, add the buttermilk mixture and blend well until the dough comes together. If you do not have a dough hook attachment, you can mix with a wooden spoon or a rubber spatula.

Increase the speed of your mixer slightly, or knead the dough by hand, until smooth and elastic. The dough will begin to pull away from the sides of the bowl. You may need to add a little more flour as you knead to keep it from becoming sticky. The total kneading time will be 6–8 minutes.

Turn the dough out onto a floured surface and knead for an additional minute. Transfer the dough to a lightly oiled bowl and cover with plastic wrap. Let rise until doubled, 1½–2 hours.

Punch down the dough and divide into 12 pieces. Shape into rolls and place on the prepared baking sheet. Cover and let rise again for 30–45 minutes, until nearly doubled in size.

While the dough is rising, preheat the oven to 350°F.

Bake until golden brown, 20–25 minutes.

Makes about 12 rolls

Cinnamon Rolls

I use the Heirloom Rolls recipe (page 100) as the basic dough for these rolls. I think the buttermilk is the magic ingredient!

1 Heirloom Rolls recipe, prepared through the first rise
½ cup butter, softened
1½ cups granulated sugar
2 teaspoons ground cinnamon

Cream Cheese Icing
4 ounces cream cheese, softened
¼ cup butter, softened
2 cups powdered sugar
¼ cup heavy cream or milk

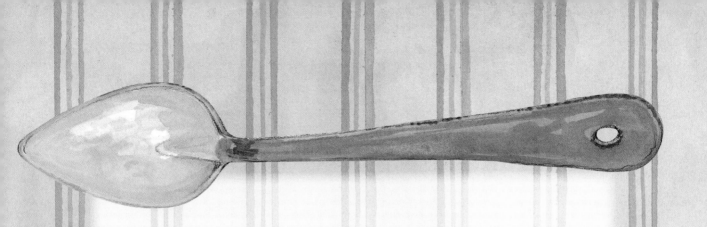

Preheat the oven to 350°F. Coat a 9 by 13-inch baking pan with nonstick cooking spray.

After the dough has risen for the first time, punch the dough down and turn onto a lightly floured work surface. Roll the dough into a 9 by 13-inch rectangle. Spread the surface of the dough with the butter. In a small bowl, combine the granulated sugar with the cinnamon, and sprinkle over the dough. Roll up, starting with the long side, pinching to seal the dough at the ends.

Cut into 12 equal pieces with a dough scraper or sharp knife. Place side by side in the prepared baking pan. Cover with plastic wrap and let rise until nearly doubled in size, 30–45 minutes.

Bake for 20–25 minutes, or until golden brown.

Prepare the icing by combining the cream cheese and butter in a mixer bowl and beating until smooth and creamy. Add the powdered sugar and continue beating until well mixed and smooth. Add the cream gradually to thin the mixture, beating for an additional 2 minutes. Spread the icing on the warm rolls before serving.

Makes 12 rolls

Banana-Chocolate Chip Bread

You know all of those scary-looking overripe bananas that everyone in the family keeps ignoring? One by one, stick those in a plastic bag in the freezer (leave the peel on if you like, though it will darken), and when you have collected 4 bananas, try this recipe for an amazing bread.

3 cups all-purpose flour

1 teaspoon baking soda

¾ teaspoon salt

3 eggs

2 cups sugar

1½ cups butter, melted

2 tablespoons vanilla extract

1½ cups mashed ripe bananas (3 or 4 medium)

½ cup buttermilk

1 cup semisweet chocolate chips

Preheat the oven to 350°F. Coat two 5 by 9-inch loaf pans with nonstick cooking spray.

In a medium bowl, whisk together the flour, baking soda, and salt and set aside.

In a large bowl, mix the eggs, sugar and melted butter until blended. Add the flour mixture to the egg mixture and stir to combine. Add the vanilla, bananas, and buttermilk and mix just until blended. Fold in ½ cup of the chocolate chips. Divide the batter evenly between the two pans. Sprinkle the remaining ½ cup chocolate chips on top of the batter in each pan. Bake for 60–65 minutes, or until a tester inserted into the center of each loaf comes out clean.

Makes 2 loaves

Loaves and Fishes

My kids and I go to a small church in the community where we live. If you were driving by, you might not even notice the sign out in front that says "Canopy . . . a church growing under grace." Those of us who started the church just wanted a name that reminded us that personal spiritual growth is both a blessing and a responsibility, and that God will provide ample grace for both.

Inside the church there is a corner set up like a small living room, with a sofa and chairs. People gather there before and after church to visit. Sometimes during church, parents with toddlers will take their restless children there to keep them from disturbing others during the service. On a table in front of the sofa, there is a giant clear canister filled with Goldfish crackers. It has a small rainbow-colored scoop inside for "fishing" out a handful of these golden snacks. Because the jar sits low on the table, it's at the perfect height for little people to see — there is hope for a treat!

Since I put the jar there when we first moved into the building, I kind of thought it would be my responsibility to keep it full. So over time, I kept my eye on it, watching everyone dip in from time to time, adults and children alike partaking. It's silly, I know, but I got a lot of pleasure watching so many people enjoy the Goldfish.

Recently I asked a fellow church friend of mine who was on her way to a big discount store to pick up a gallon-size box of Goldfish for me to replenish our supply. When I tried to pay her for them, she said, "Please let me fill the jar this time." Month after month, I've never seen the jar empty, in spite of the rainbow scoop regularly moving in and moving out. There always seems to be more than enough.

The Goldfish jar as a metaphor for life has become kind of a sweet symbol for me: a symbol of care, generosity, and trust — even a promise of abundance and fun. I believe that years from now, whether I am around or not, there will still be plenty of Goldfish in the jar.

Go fish.

Canopy

Desserts

Fruit Pizza

I've enjoyed other versions of this dessert before, but I have to boast that all of them pale in comparison to this recipe. It's the cookie crust that makes the difference. My daughter and I had two of our favorite friends over one evening to experiment in the kitchen, and we all agreed that this treat was at the top of our list of favorites. Thank you to Hailey and Sherri Claunch for your diligent dishwashing all night long!

½ cup margarine, softened

½ cup butter, softened

1½ cups sugar

2 eggs

2 teaspoons cream of tartar

1 teaspoon baking soda

1 teaspoon vanilla extract

2¾ cups all-purpose flour

2 (8-ounce) packages cream cheese, softened

¼ cup freshly squeezed orange juice

Assorted fruits: We used sliced strawberries, chopped fresh pineapple, and apple slices. Other options include kiwi, raspberries, or blueberries.

Preheat the oven to 400°F. Coat a 10 by 15-inch jelly-roll pan with non-stick cooking spray.

Cream the margarine, butter, and 1 cup of the sugar together until light and fluffy, about 1 minute. Add the eggs, cream of tartar, baking soda, vanilla, and flour. Mix well. Transfer the dough onto the prepared baking pan. Bake for 10 minutes. Set aside to cool.

Using a standing mixer with a paddle attachment, beat the cream cheese, the remaining ½ cup of sugar, and the juice together until smooth, about 1 minute. Spread the filling on the cooled crust. Slice assorted fruits and arrange artfully on top of the filling. Cover and chill until ready to serve.

Serves 10–12

PB and J BARS

This delicious recipe comes together quickly, but you'll want to allow several hours for the bars to cool before cutting into serving-size pieces. Feel free to substitute any flavor jam or jelly.

1 cup butter, softened

1½ cups sugar

2 eggs

1 (18-ounce) jar creamy peanut butter

3 cups all-purpose flour

1 teaspoon salt

1 teaspoon baking powder

1 teaspoon vanilla extract

1½ cups grape jam or jelly

Yum!

Preheat the oven to 350°F. Coat a 9 by 13-inch baking dish with nonstick cooking spray.

In a mixer bowl, cream the butter and sugar together until light and fluffy, about 2 minutes. Add the eggs and peanut butter, beating well after each addition. In a medium bowl, whisk together the flour, salt, and baking powder. Add the dry ingredients to the butter mixture, and beat on low speed until combined. Add the vanilla and mix well.

Transfer two-thirds of the mixture to the prepared baking dish, spreading evenly over the bottom of the dish. Spread the jam on top of the peanut butter mixture. Crumble the remaining one-third of the dough over the jam.

Bake until golden, 45–55 minutes. Cool on a wire rack for at least 1 hour before cutting into bars.

Makes 2 dozen bars

Lisa's Bliss Bars

Lisa Black-Schwandt is one of the many amazing teachers here in our lake area. When she brought this recipe by our store for our staff to sample, we all agreed that this recipe had to be included in the next cookbook.

2 cups all-purpose flour

1½ cups quick-cooking oats

¾ cup firmly packed brown sugar, plus 1 tablespoon

1 cup butter, softened

1 (8-ounce) package cream cheese, softened

1 (14-ounce) can sweetened condensed milk

¼ cup freshly squeezed lemon juice

1 teaspoon vanilla extract

2 tablespoons cornstarch

1 (21-ounce) can whole-berry cranberry sauce

Preheat the oven to 350°F. Coat a 9 by 13-inch baking dish with nonstick cooking spray.

In a large bowl, combine the flour, oats, ¾ cup of the brown sugar, and the butter. Using a fork, mix until crumbly. Set aside 1½ cups of this crumb mixture for the topping. Press the remaining crumb mixture into the bottom of the prepared baking dish. Bake for 15 minutes. Cool completely.

In a large mixer bowl, beat the cream cheese until smooth, gradually adding the condensed milk, lemon juice, and vanilla. Beat until smooth. Pour this mixture evenly over the cooled crust.

In a small bowl, combine the remaining 1 tablespoon brown sugar with the cornstarch and cranberry sauce. Mix well and spoon over the cream cheese mixture.

Sprinkle the reserved crumb mixture over the top. Bake for 40 minutes, or until golden brown. Cool completely. Refrigerate for 30 minutes before cutting into bars to serve.

Serves 12

BROOKE'S BLONDE ROCKIES

This cookie bar is really more like a candy bar than a cookie. My daughter made these for her track buddies and they were a big hit.

2 ¼ cups all-purpose flour

2 ¼ teaspoons baking powder

1 teaspoon salt

½ cup butter, softened

1½ cups firmly packed brown sugar

3 eggs

1 teaspoon vanilla extract

1 cup miniature marshmallows

2 cups semisweet chocolate chips

1 cup white chocolate chips

½ cup chopped pecans (optional)

½ cup caramel ice cream topping (optional)

Preheat the oven to 350°F. Coat a 9 by 13-inch baking dish with nonstick cooking spray.

Whisk together the flour, baking powder, and salt in a medium bowl. In a large mixer bowl, cream the butter and brown sugar together until fluffy, about 1 minute. Add the eggs and vanilla and mix well. Stir in the flour mixture until well combined. Fold in ½ cup of the marshmallows, 1 cup of the chocolate chips, and ½ cup of the white chocolate chips.

Spread the dough in the prepared baking dish. Scatter the remaining ½ cup marshmallows, 1 cup chocolate chips, and ½ cup white chocolate chips over the top of the dough. Bake for about 35 minutes, or until a tester inserted in the center comes out clean. If you like, sprinkle the pecans over the top and drizzle with the caramel topping. Cool completely, and then cut into squares or triangles.

Serves 12

Roxie's Orange Sugar Cookies

If you are looking for a cookie that is light but satisfying, try this. It's a great picnic or brunch treat.

½ cup butter, softened

1½ cups sugar

½ teaspoon salt

1½ teaspoons grated orange peel

1 egg

2 tablespoons freshly squeezed orange juice

2 cups all-purpose flour

1 teaspoon baking powder

½ teaspoon baking soda

½ cup dried cranberries

½ cup broken nuts (pecans or walnuts are good)

1 teaspoon ground cinnamon or nutmeg

Preheat the oven to 375°F.

In a mixer bowl, cream the butter, 1 cup of the sugar, the salt, and the orange peel together. Mix until light and fluffy, about 1 minute.

Beat in the egg and orange juice. Add the flour, baking powder, and baking soda. Blend into the butter mixture until well combined. Fold in the cranberries and nuts. Chill for at least 20 minutes.

Combine the remaining ½ cup sugar and the cinnamon in a shallow bowl. Using a 1½-inch cookie scoop, scoop out some dough and drop into the cinnamon-sugar mixture. Roll the dough in the mixture and place the pieces 2 inches apart on an ungreased baking sheet. Bake for 8–10 minutes, or until very lightly browned. Cool on a wire rack.

Makes 2½ dozen cookies

Melt-in-Your-Mouth Cookies

Seriously, these cookies _do_ melt in your mouth. I usually divide the dough in half and bake half without pecans. And the other half is baked with a pecan half pressed into the center of the top of each cookie. Either way, they are luscious!

1 cup granulated sugar

1 cup butter, softened

2 eggs

1 cup vegetable oil

2 teaspoons vanilla extract

4½ cups all-purpose flour

½ teaspoon salt

1 teaspoon baking soda

½ teaspoon cream of tartar

1 cup shredded coconut

1 cup powdered sugar

½ cup pecan halves (optional)

m.. ..m.. ..m!

Preheat the oven to 350°F.

In the bowl of an electric mixer, cream the sugar and butter together until light and fluffy, about 1 minute. Add the eggs, vegetable oil, and vanilla and mix well.

In a large bowl, combine the flour, salt, baking soda, and cream of tartar. Whisk to mix well. Add the flour mixture to the butter mixture and blend well. Add the coconut and mix well again. Chill the dough for at least 2 hours to make handling easier.

Place the powdered sugar on a dinner plate or a large sheet of waxed paper. Using a 1½-inch cookie scoop, scoop out the dough and gently roll each scoop of dough to completely cover it with the powdered sugar. Transfer each scoop to an ungreased baking sheet, placing them at least 2 inches apart. If you like, press a pecan half into the center of half of the cookies. Bake for 10–12 minutes, or until set but not brown.

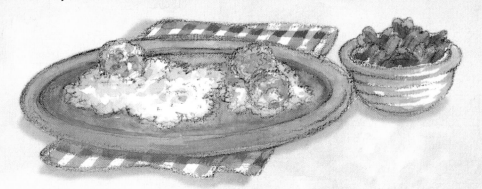

Makes 4½ dozen cookies

Caramel Oatmeal Bars

This is a great recipe for beginning bakers, since there are so few ingredients and a minimum number of steps. Children love making <u>and</u> eating these yummy cookie bars.

1 (18½-ounce) package yellow cake mix
2½ cups quick-cooking oats
¾ cup butter, melted
2 cups semisweet chocolate chips
1 (8-ounce) jar caramel ice cream topping

Delicious! ♡

Preheat the oven to 375°F. Coat a 9 by 13-inch baking dish with nonstick cooking spray.

In a large bowl, stir together the cake mix and oats. Stir in the butter with a fork until the mixture is crumbly and the dry ingredients are moistened. Press half of this mixture evenly into the bottom of the prepared baking dish. Sprinkle the chocolate chips evenly over this mixture and top with the remaining oat mixture.

Bake for 30 minutes, or until golden brown. Drizzle the caramel evenly over the top of the baked bars. Let cool before slicing into bars.

Makes 2 dozen bars

Lunch Box Brownies

What I love most about this recipe is the simplicity of the ingredients list. No extravagant expensive groceries required! Very few tools are needed to pull this quick treat together — you don't even need a mixer. I think your family and friends will begin to think of this recipe as one of those "tried and true" desserts.

1 cup butter

⅔ cup semisweet chocolate chips

1¾ cups sugar

¼ teaspoon salt

1 cup all-purpose flour

4 eggs

1 teaspoon vanilla extract

1 cup broken nuts (I prefer English walnuts or pecans for this recipe)

Preheat the oven to 325°F. Line 10 jumbo muffin cups with large paper liners. Melt the butter and chocolate chips in a large microwave-safe bowl in the microwave. This will take 60–90 seconds. Stir until smooth. Add the sugar, salt, and flour. Mix until just blended. Add the eggs, one at a time, mixing but not beating after each. Stir in the vanilla and nuts. Fill each muffin cup about two-thirds full. Bake for 25–30 minutes, or until set. Be careful not to overbake!

Makes 10 large brownies

peanut butter blondies

This blond beauty has a very subtle peanut butter flavor and is a close cousin in many ways to my Lunch Box Brownies (page 121). The ingredients and texture are very similar, and they are both chewy and dense. I love that they are so portable. You can serve them warm with ice cream right out of the oven, or as a simple lunch box treat.

1 cup butter

⅔ cup peanut butter chips

1¾ cups sugar

¼ teaspoon salt

1 cup all-purpose flour

4 eggs

1 teaspoon vanilla extract

1 cup semisweet chocolate chips

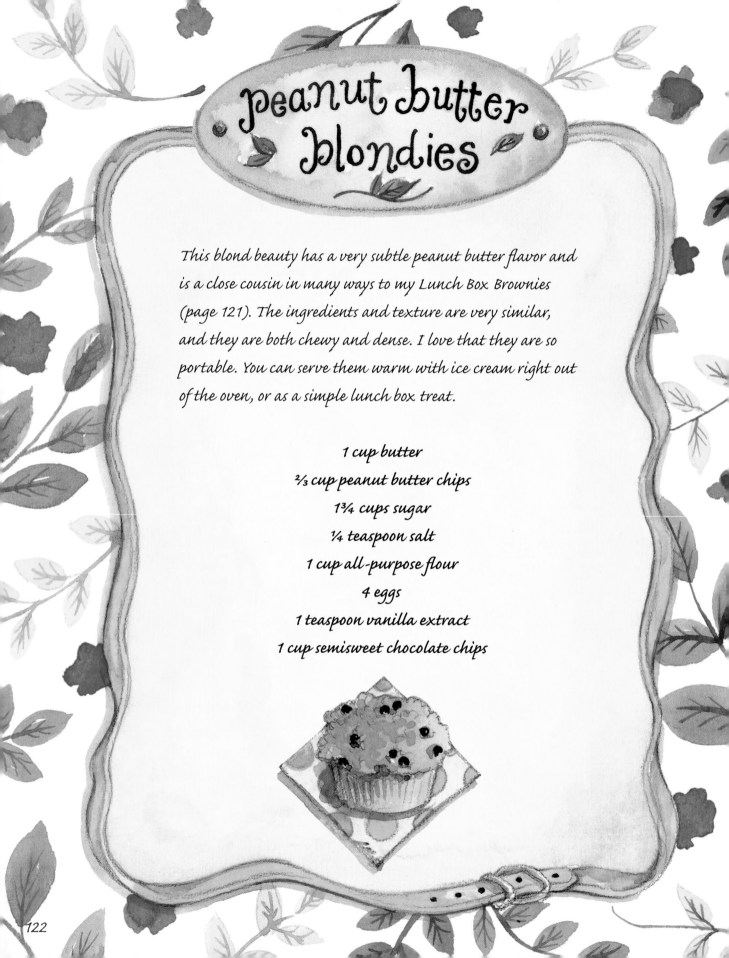

Preheat the oven to 325°F. Line jumbo muffin cups with paper liners.

Melt the butter and peanut butter chips in a large microwave-safe bowl in the microwave. This will take 60–90 seconds. Stir until smooth. Beat in the sugar, salt, and flour. Add the eggs, one at a time, stirring but not beating after each. Add the vanilla and ½ cup of the chocolate chips. Fill the muffin cups about two-thirds full. Divide the remaining ½ cup of the chocolate chips over the top of each blondie. Bake for 25–30 minutes, or until set. Be careful not to overbake!

Makes 8–10 blondies

Not Fried Ice Cream

This is another sweet treat from my special friends Kate and Maureen (mother and daughter). You'll love being able to prepare these a day or so in advance of a special celebration, knowing that the dessert work is behind you!

½ gallon vanilla ice cream
¼ cup butter
½ cup all-purpose flour
⅓ cup shredded coconut
⅓ cup chopped pecans
1 tablespoon brown sugar
½ teaspoon ground cinnamon
1 cup caramel ice cream topping
3 tablespoons Kahlúa or other coffee liqueur (optional)

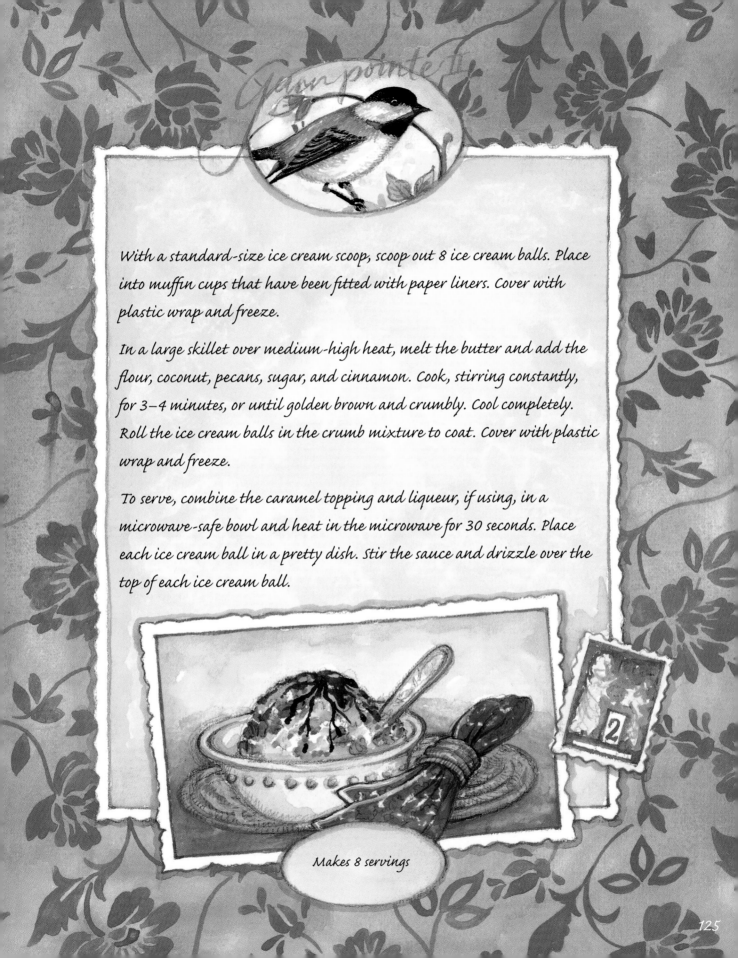

With a standard-size ice cream scoop, scoop out 8 ice cream balls. Place into muffin cups that have been fitted with paper liners. Cover with plastic wrap and freeze.

In a large skillet over medium-high heat, melt the butter and add the flour, coconut, pecans, sugar, and cinnamon. Cook, stirring constantly, for 3–4 minutes, or until golden brown and crumbly. Cool completely. Roll the ice cream balls in the crumb mixture to coat. Cover with plastic wrap and freeze.

To serve, combine the caramel topping and liqueur, if using, in a microwave-safe bowl and heat in the microwave for 30 seconds. Place each ice cream ball in a pretty dish. Stir the sauce and drizzle over the top of each ice cream ball.

Makes 8 servings

Chocolate Cheesecake

This cheesecake, baked in a pie dish, can be prepared very quickly, but it does require chilling after baking for at least 4 hours or overnight. For that reason, it's a great make-ahead dish! You can also make it a little extra-special by garnishing it after slicing with a variety of things: toasted coconut and pecans, chocolate and/or caramel ice cream topping, etc. If you're fond of banana splits, try topping it with sliced bananas, strawberries, and crushed pineapple with a little chocolate sauce and whipped cream.

Crust

5 tablespoons butter

1⅓ cups graham cracker crumbs

3 tablespoons sugar

Filling

4 (1-ounce) squares semisweet baking chocolate

2 (8-ounce) packages cream cheese, softened

½ cup sugar

1 tablespoon all-purpose flour

½ teaspoon vanilla extract

2 eggs

Toppings of your choice
(see suggestions at the beginning of the recipe)

Preheat the oven to 325°F.

To make the crust, in a medium microwave-safe bowl, melt the butter in the microwave. This will take about 30 seconds. Add the graham cracker crumbs and sugar. Mix well and turn into a 9-inch pie pan or dish. Press evenly into the bottom of the pan. Bake for 5 minutes. Set aside to cool.

To make the filling, heat the chocolate in a small microwave-safe bowl at 50 percent power for 60–90 seconds, or until melted, stirring midway through the heating process. Let cool slightly.

In a large mixing bowl, blend the cream cheese, sugar, flour, and vanilla until smooth. Add the chocolate and mix until well combined. Add the eggs, one at a time, and mix on low speed until just blended.

Pour into the prepared pie crust and bake for 45–50 minutes, or until set. Cool. Cover and refrigerate for at least 4 hours before serving. Garnish with the toppings of your choice.

Makes 8–10 servings

Pumpkin Cheesecake

If you're looking for a great make-ahead dessert, this could be the perfect solution. If I've planned to have company for dinner, I like to prepare this recipe the night before, making the other preparations so much more enjoyable and less stressful.

30 gingersnap cookies, crushed

6 tablespoons butter, melted

4 (8-ounce) packages cream cheese, softened

1 cup sugar

1 teaspoon vanilla extract

4 eggs

1 cup canned pumpkin

1 teaspoon ground cinnamon

¼ teaspoon ground nutmeg

Dash of ground cloves

Whipped cream, for garnish

Preheat the oven to 315°F.

Mix the gingersnaps and butter in a small bowl and press evenly into the bottom of a 9-inch springform pan.

Beat the cream cheese, ¾ cup of the sugar, and the vanilla with an electric mixer until well blended. Add the eggs, one at a time, mixing on low speed just until blended. Remove 2 cups of the batter; place in a small bowl and set aside. Stir the remaining ¼ cup of sugar, the pumpkin, cinnamon, nutmeg, and cloves into the remaining batter. Spoon half of the pumpkin batter into the crust; top with the reserved plain batter. Add the remaining pumpkin batter on top and cut through the batters with a knife to create a marbled effect.

Bake for 60–65 minutes, or until the center is set. Cool before removing the rim of the pan. Refrigerate for at least 3 hours before serving. Top with a generous amount of whipped cream just before serving.

Makes 10–12 servings

Earthquake Cake

This is a very rich cake, loved by everyone who sampled it!

1 cup chopped pecans

1 cup shredded coconut

1 (18¼-ounce) box German chocolate cake mix

Eggs, vegetable oil, and water in quantities
according to cake mix directions

1 (1-pound) box powdered sugar

½ cup butter, softened

1 (8-ounce) package cream cheese, softened

1 teaspoon vanilla extract

Preheat the oven to 350°F. Coat a 9 by 13-inch baking dish with nonstick cooking spray.

Scatter the nuts and coconut in the bottom of the baking dish. In a mixer bowl, prepare the cake mix according to the package directions. Pour the cake mixture over the nuts and coconut. There is no need to stir.

In a mixer bowl, combine the powdered sugar, butter, cream cheese, and vanilla. Mix until well blended, about 2 minutes. Spoon this mixture over the top of the cake batter. Do not stir. Bake for 45–50 minutes, or until cracks appear in the cake. Cool slightly before cutting and serving.

Makes 12 servings

Apple Squares

One of the nice things about this dessert is its "petite-ness." If you have a small gathering of family or friends and don't need the temptation of sweet leftovers lingering in your kitchen for days, this might be the recipe for you.

1 cup butter, plus 2 tablespoons

1½ cups sugar

3 eggs

¼ teaspoon salt

2 teaspoons baking powder

2 cups all-purpose flour

4 Granny Smith apples, peeled and sliced

2 teaspoons ground cinnamon

Preheat the oven to 350°F. Spray an 8-inch or 10-inch square baking pan with nonstick cooking spray.

Cream 1 cup of the butter and 1 cup of the sugar together in a large bowl until light and fluffy, about 1 minute. Add the eggs, one at a time, beating well after each. Add the salt, baking powder, and flour. Beat until smooth. Put one-half of the batter in the prepared pan. Cover with the apples. Combine the remaining ½ cup of sugar with the cinnamon and sprinkle over the top of the apples. Dot with the remaining 2 tablespoons of butter. Cover with the remaining batter. Bake for 30–40 minutes, until golden brown.

Makes 4–6 servings

Cranberry-Orange Coffeecake

I don't know if this ever happens to you, but I got completely addicted to this coffeecake last winter. At first I kept making it because I was trying to fine-tune the recipe. But even after I was satisfied with the recipe, I just kept craving it! So proceed with caution. I am now spending extra time at the gym, suffering the consequences of my addiction.

1 orange

1 (18¼-ounce) box yellow cake mix

Eggs and vegetable oil in quantities
according to cake mix directions

1 (12-ounce) package fresh or frozen cranberries

1 cup chopped pecans or walnuts

½ cup firmly packed brown sugar

1 teaspoon ground cinnamon

1 cup powdered sugar

2 tablespoons water

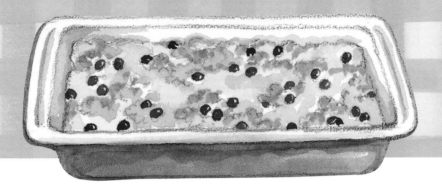

Preheat the oven to 350°F. Coat a 9 by 13-inch baking dish with nonstick cooking spray.

Using a zester, scrape the orange peel to yield 1 tablespoon of orange zest. Set aside. Then slice the orange in half and squeeze out as much juice as possible into a measuring cup. Discard any seeds that might have fallen into the measuring cup. Reserve 2 tablespoons orange juice to be used later in the glaze.

Prepare the cake mix according to the directions on the box, using the fresh orange juice combined with enough water to equal the amount of water called for in the directions. Add the orange zest and mix well. Fold in half of the cranberries. Spread the batter into the prepared baking dish. Sprinkle the remaining cranberries over the top of the batter.

Combine the pecans, brown sugar, and cinnamon. Sprinkle evenly over the top of the batter. Bake for 35–40 minutes, or until a tester inserted in the center comes out clean.

Combine the powdered sugar, the reserved 2 tablespoons orange juice, and the water. Beat until smooth. Drizzle this glaze over the top of the warm cake.

Makes 12 servings

Pecan Fudge Sheet Cake with Fudge Frosting

If there is an occasion when you need a quick fix for a major chocolate craving, this simple recipe could be just the solution. There is a very good chance that you'll have most, if not all, of these ingredients on hand. If you like, instead of the frosting, you may dust the cake with powdered sugar before serving.

2 cups sugar

1 cup butter, softened

2 eggs

1 teaspoon vanilla extract

2 cups all-purpose flour

½ teaspoon salt

1 teaspoon baking soda

⅓ cup cocoa

½ cup sour cream

½ cup buttermilk (or 1 tablespoon white vinegar added to enough milk to measure ½ cup)

1 cup chopped pecans

Preheat the oven to 350°F. Coat a 10 x 17-inch sheet cake pan with non-stick cooking spray.

Cream the sugar and butter together in a large bowl until light, about 1 minute. Add the eggs and vanilla, beating until smooth.

In a separate bowl, stir together the flour, salt, baking soda, and cocoa. Combine the sour cream and buttermilk in a small bowl.

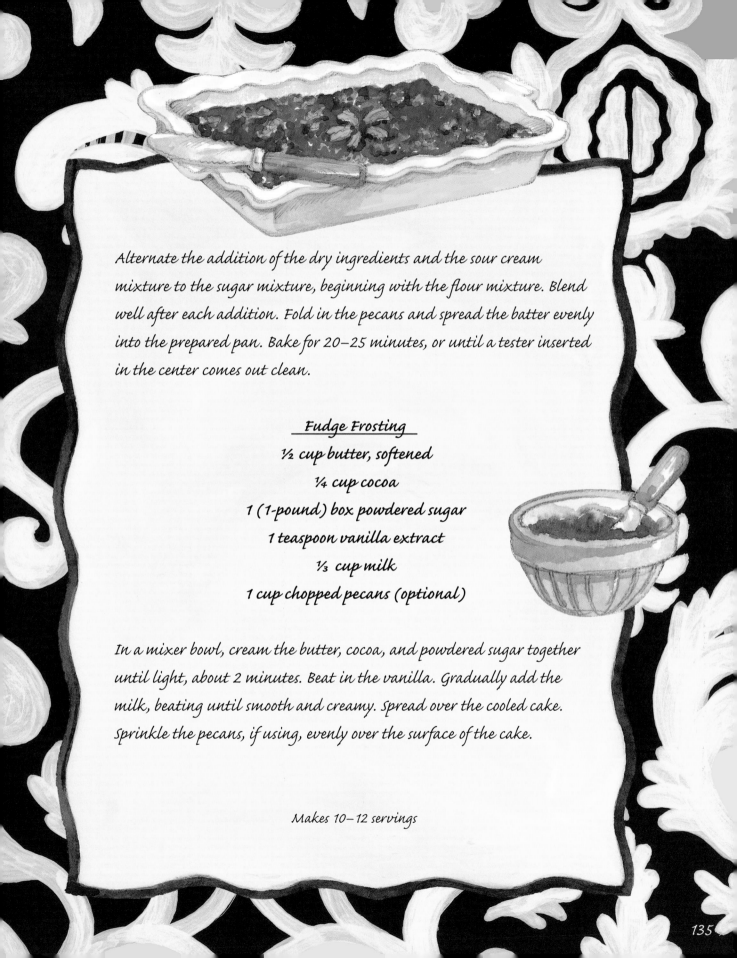

Alternate the addition of the dry ingredients and the sour cream mixture to the sugar mixture, beginning with the flour mixture. Blend well after each addition. Fold in the pecans and spread the batter evenly into the prepared pan. Bake for 20–25 minutes, or until a tester inserted in the center comes out clean.

Fudge Frosting
½ cup butter, softened

¼ cup cocoa

1 (1-pound) box powdered sugar

1 teaspoon vanilla extract

⅓ cup milk

1 cup chopped pecans (optional)

In a mixer bowl, cream the butter, cocoa, and powdered sugar together until light, about 2 minutes. Beat in the vanilla. Gradually add the milk, beating until smooth and creamy. Spread over the cooled cake. Sprinkle the pecans, if using, evenly over the surface of the cake.

Makes 10–12 servings

fast fondue

I love this simple recipe for chocolate fondue! I've used it dozens of times and it always gets rave reviews. In less than an hour, it will be possible for you to have everything ready for a really fun fondue party. I'm listing my favorite foods for dipping, but you may have other ideas to give this recipe your own personal touch.

1 cup heavy cream or half-and-half
1½ cups semisweet chocolate chips
1 (12-ounce) milk chocolate bar, broken into pieces
½ cup butter

Foods for dipping:
Pound cake and/or angel food cake, cut into cubes
Cheesecake bites
Brownies, cut into 1-inch squares
Fresh fruit, cut into chunks (strawberries, bananas, and fresh pineapple are good choices)
Pretzels
Nuts
Marshmallows
Cookies

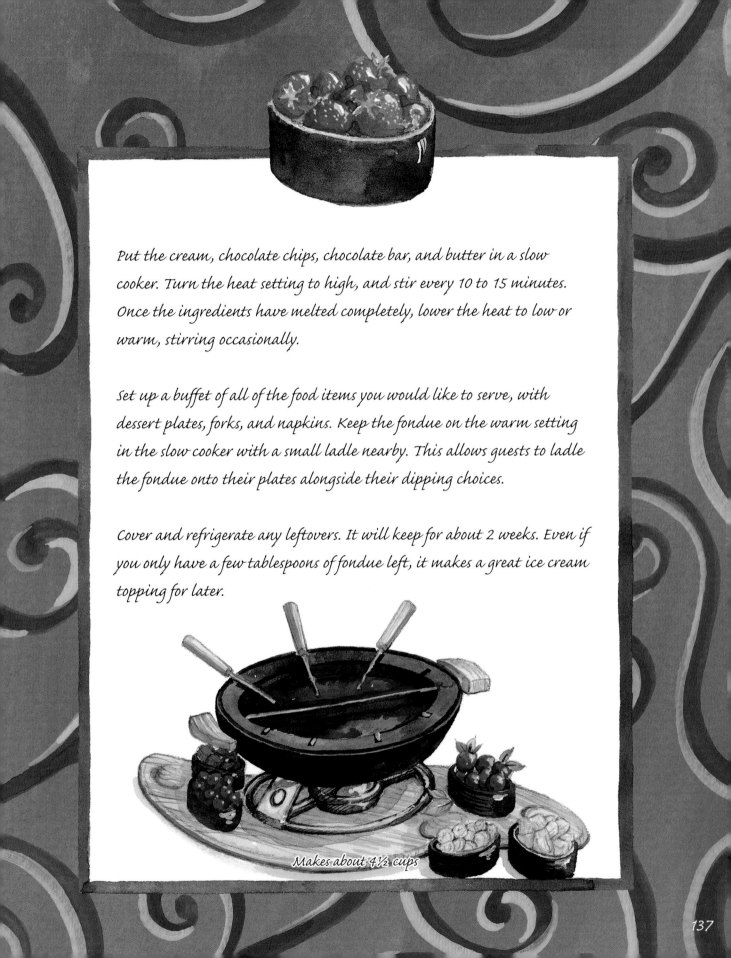

Put the cream, chocolate chips, chocolate bar, and butter in a slow cooker. Turn the heat setting to high, and stir every 10 to 15 minutes. Once the ingredients have melted completely, lower the heat to low or warm, stirring occasionally.

Set up a buffet of all of the food items you would like to serve, with dessert plates, forks, and napkins. Keep the fondue on the warm setting in the slow cooker with a small ladle nearby. This allows guests to ladle the fondue onto their plates alongside their dipping choices.

Cover and refrigerate any leftovers. It will keep for about 2 weeks. Even if you only have a few tablespoons of fondue left, it makes a great ice cream topping for later.

Makes about 4½ cups

Jan's Just "Dew" It Apple Dessert

It's very fitting that my sister, Jan, would share this recipe with me. It's a lot like her — sweet, full of good stuff, a little nutty, and _fun_. You will love surprising your friends and family with this dessert. It is _amazing_ served warm with ice cream.

2 (8-ounce) packages refrigerated crescent roll dough
2 Granny Smith apples, peeled, cored, and cut into 8 wedges
1 cup butter, melted
1 cup sugar
1½ teaspoons ground cinnamon
1 cup English walnuts
1 (12-ounce) can Mountain Dew
1 gallon vanilla ice cream, for serving

Preheat the oven to 350°F. Coat a 9 by 13-inch baking dish with nonstick cooking spray.

Separate the crescent roll dough into triangles and roll 1 wedge of apple into each triangle. Place the apple rolls side by side in the prepared pan.

Combine the melted butter with the sugar and cinnamon.

Pour this mixture over the top of the rolls. Sprinkle the walnuts evenly over the top. Pour the can of Mountain Dew over all.

Bake for 45–50 minutes, until golden brown. Serve warm with ice cream.

Makes 8–10 servings

Solitary Refinement

Perhaps as you're enjoying Shelly's amazing artwork in this book, you're wondering, "How does this more-time-at-the-table theme relate to me, someone who lives alone?"

Believe me, with one son in college and a daughter who will also be there by the time you hold this book in your hands, I've thought about that. I've starting picturing myself, sitting there alone, and I can tell you it's not a vision I'm happy about.

So what do we do about that? Don't we still need all of those things the table has come to represent to us? How can our needs still be met in our solitude?

One of the table traditions my children and I have shared through the years is called "High-Low." I'm sure there are other families who have a similar activity at the table. It works like this: Each person around the table recounts the highest point of his or her day, and also the lowest point. You can learn so much from this shared experience. When we have had guests and their turn comes around, it's incredible how many of them respond, "My high is this — right here and now, being with you." That remark inspires me to never take this time for granted.

In the absence of my family, I plan to regularly extend this simple invitation to my friends: "Would you have dinner with me?" But if there are no takers, I promise to pull up a chair to my treasured table, use my napkin, and bow my head in thanks. I pledge to rejoice in the highs and not dwell too long on the lows. Will you join me?

For each new morning
with its light,
For rest and shelter of the night,
For health and food, for love and friends,
For everything Thy goodness sends.
— Ralph Waldo Emerson

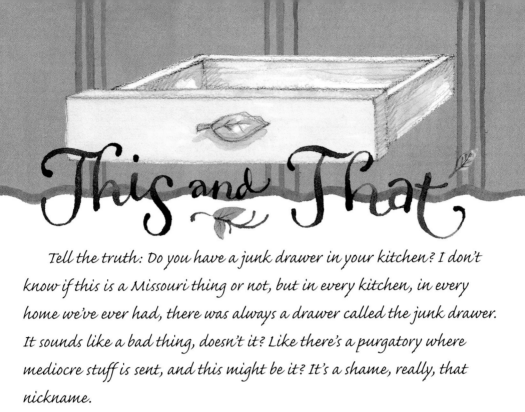

This and That

Tell the truth: Do you have a junk drawer in your kitchen? I don't know if this is a Missouri thing or not, but in every kitchen, in every home we've ever had, there was always a drawer called the junk drawer. It sounds like a bad thing, doesn't it? Like there's a purgatory where mediocre stuff is sent, and this might be it? It's a shame, really, that nickname.

It's a shame because there are some real treasures in our junk drawer: second sets of car keys, order forms for school pictures, thirty-nine-cent stamps, coupons, extra pens, a screwdriver, a few pieces of (wrapped, thank goodness!) dark chocolate, and half a package of gum.

When you're setting up house after a move or doing some spring cleaning, and you've organized your kitchen the best you can, there is inevitably a pile of stuff left on the counter that just doesn't belong in any of the other drawers or cabinets. That's what this chapter is about: valuable stuff that doesn't belong in the other chapters. If you find "This and That" to be a little (shall we say) on the random side, picture your junk drawer and hold it in high esteem.

Maurice's Holiday Tea

Maurice McNabb is a longtime friend and an excellent cook. It makes sense that Maurice, as a retired art teacher, would come up with a recipe that is so visually appealing! This tea recipe is great for a large crowd.

1 gallon brewed black tea

12 whole cloves

1 (1-pound) package cinnamon Red Hots candies

2 quarts apple juice

2 quarts cranberry juice

1 (12-ounce) can frozen orange juice concentrate

1 (6-ounce) package cherry Jell-O

Bring all of the ingredients to a boil in a very large stockpot. Heat through until all the candy has dissolved. Lower the heat and simmer until ready to serve. Serve hot.

Note: This can be made ahead of time and kept in the freezer until you need it. Maurice uses empty milk jugs to store the tea. It can be frozen for up to 2 months. Allow 4 hours to thaw before reheating to serve.

Makes about 3 gallons

House of Grace Tea

Dee Stoelting uses this tea recipe for many of her catered events. It's a refreshing blend of flavors and a nice alternative in place of punch.

16 teaspoons powdered instant tea mix
2 cups sugar
1 cup freshly squeezed lemon juice
2 cups white grape juice

Mix all of the ingredients together in a large pitcher. Add enough water to make 1 gallon. Chill and serve. Leftover tea will keep in the refrigerator for up to 2 weeks.

Makes 1 gallon

Christine's Marinade

On a beautiful early summer evening last year my good friend Christine Klieber treated me to a tasty meal at her home here at the lake. Besides the gift of her time, she shared so much: a hilarious account of her labor experience (as in the giving-birth kind of labor), amazing stories of raising her just-about-perfect daughter Katie, a few gardening tips, and this simple marinade recipe. I wish everyone could be blessed with a friend like Chris.

Use this marinade with chicken, pork, or beef.

½ cup soy sauce

½ cup balsamic vinegar

½ cup olive oil

½ cup honey

2 cloves garlic, minced

Salt and freshly ground black pepper

Blend the soy sauce, vinegar, olive oil, and honey together, beating well with a whisk. Make sure to add the ingredients in this order, so that the honey will just slide out of the measuring cup where the oil has just been. Then add the garlic and the salt and pepper. Place the marinade inside a large zip-top plastic bag. Then place the bag into a bowl to prevent leaking.

Note: Allow your meat or poultry to marinate for at least an hour. After you remove the meat or poultry from the bag, discard the marinade.

Makes 2 cups, enough for 4–6 servings

Lance's Pork and Poultry Marinade

A special thank-you to the Foulk family for opening their home to us on so many different occasions. I imagine that when Lance makes this marinade for his family, he is using honey from their own bees. That which is sweet becomes sweeter!

½ cup honey

¼ cup Dijon mustard (any mustard will work)

¼ cup freshly squeezed citrus juice of your choice

¼ cup soy sauce

1 or 2 cloves garlic, crushed

Combine all the ingredients and blend well. Reserve ¾ cup of the marinade and pour the rest over the pork or poultry of your choice inside a zip-top plastic bag. Marinate for at least 2 hours or overnight. Refrigerate the reserved marinade.

When ready to cook or grill, remove the pork or poultry from the bag and discard the marinade in the bag.

While cooking or grilling the pork or poultry, bring the reserved marinade to a boil in a heavy saucepan. Lower the heat and keep warm until dinnertime. Pour over the pork or poultry right before serving.

Makes about 1¼ cups, enough for 4 servings

Bread Crumb Blend

This is such a very simple thing, but I love having this mixture on hand. I use it in place of plain dry bread crumbs when coating chicken or fish. It can also be used in some vegetable or potato recipes where bread crumbs are used as a topping. It just adds a little extra flavor — I think you'll enjoy this.

36 butter-flavored crackers
1 cup dry bread crumbs

Place the crackers inside a heavy-duty zip-top plastic bag. Press out most of the air and seal almost shut, leaving about a ½-inch opening at the top. Using a rolling pin, crush the crackers until they are uniformly fine. Add the bread crumbs to the bag. Seal and shake to mix well. Store in an airtight container for up to 3 months.

Makes 2 cups

Toasting Nuts

Nuts are most flavorful when they are toasted! There are several different ways to do this. Here are a few options:

In a Skillet

Put up to 1 cup of nuts or seeds in a dry skillet over medium heat. Shake the skillet occasionally to prevent scorching and toast them until they are lightly browned and fragrant. This will take only 5 or 6 minutes.

In the Oven

Preheat the oven to 350°F. Put up to 3 cups of nuts or seeds on a heavy baking sheet. Spread them out in a single layer. Toast the nuts, shaking the pan after a few minutes. Continue toasting for an additional 5–8 minutes, until they are lightly browned and fragrant.

In the Microwave

Place up to 1 cup of nuts or seeds in a single layer in a shallow glass pie plate. Microwave on high for 3–4 minutes, until they are lightly browned. Shake every minute to be sure they brown evenly.

We're Talking Tools

I've often thought that if I ever had to quit my day job, I could become a successful kitchen gadget salesperson. That's how devoted I am to my favorite tools and appliances. When I sold my restaurant after running it for 8 years, I had a very difficult time leaving my knives behind, not to mention my blessed KitchenAid mixer. I was only able to do so by promising myself that I would immediately replace them the instant I drove out of the parking lot for the last time. So you can see I'm serious about this subject.

I do have some favorite brands, but I will try to give you a good basic list of the things I've found to be helpful through the years. You can add these things to your kitchen gradually over time. This list will in no way include everything I've found to be useful — these are just a few of my personal favorites.

If you are as passionate about your tools as I am, there are some fun things you can do to share your passion.

One of the traditions I've started with my children is randomly giving them a gift of a tool, accompanied with a lesson on how to use it and care for it. I've also tied tools to wrapped gifts and stuffed them in Christmas stockings. Speaking of Christmas, you could give a Christmas tree decorated with tools instead of ornaments to young cooks stepping out on their own for the first time in their lives. So, let's talk about some of my favorites.

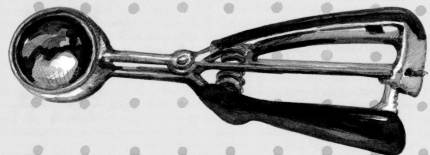

Bowl Scraper

There are many different kinds of scrapers. My favorite is made of plastic with one straight side and one curved side. The curved side is perfect for scraping batter or dough from a bowl, and the straight side is helpful when transferring chopped vegetables from a work surface into a pot or bowl.

Chopping Mat

You can't even imagine how excited I was to see the arrival of flexible plastic chopping mats to our collection of cooking aids. They seemed almost too good to be true! Priced at about a dollar each, they are perfect for slicing and dicing almost anything, and some are even dishwasher safe. You can use them like a funnel for transferring cut-up food, keeping messes to a minimum. You can also draw ruler measurements on the back of the clear mats with a permanent marker for assistance in slicing more precisely. If you haven't discovered these mats yet, I predict you'll love them.

Because the plastic chopping mats are so inexpensive, you can purchase several and designate one for vegetables, one for poultry, one for fish, etc. This helps to cut down on the possibility of cross contamination. Depending on how much you use your mats, you may want to replace them every year or so.

Cookie Scoop

A cookie scoop is really just a slightly smaller than usual ice cream scoop with a release mechanism. They are available in graduated sizes. I have a very small one that I use for tea cookies, but the one I use the most is 1½ inches in diameter. It's not only helpful in keeping cookies uniform in size but it's also great for filling miniature muffin tins with batter.

Dough Scraper

A dough scraper, also known as a bench scraper, is usually made of metal or plastic, and is used to clean scraps of dough from the work surface. It is also very handy in scoring and/or cutting dough. And, like its cousin, the bowl scraper, you can use it like a flat scoop when you have large amounts of cut vegetables to transfer from the counter to pots and bowls.

Kitchen Shears

I use my kitchen shears nearly every time I cook. Some favorite uses: cutting slashes into shaped bread dough, snipping slices of bacon into small pieces, cutting up canned whole tomatoes (leave them in the can and cut away), cutting garlic bread into serving-size pieces, and mincing fresh herbs. Some shears have break-apart blades that separate at the fulcrum for ease in cleaning.

Knives

Last on my list, but certainly not least in importance, are knives. I mostly prefer knives with rubber handles, which make gripping easier and safer, and high-carbon stainless steel blades. There are so many different sizes and styles, each serving a specific purpose in cutting and carving. But it's very difficult to prepare even the most basic recipes without having the following three types in your kitchen.

Chef's Knife — This is probably the most useful tool you will own. It's perfect for mincing herbs, chopping vegetables, and slicing fruit. Test the feel of the handle in your hand. A slightly curved blade will make mincing a little easier.

Paring Knife — Use this knife for peeling, coring, and slicing fruits and vegetables. It should have a handle that fits your hand, with a little flexibility in the blade.

Bread Knife — My favorite bread knife is actually made completely of plastic. It has a long blade with a serrated edge. I purchased it for about $3.00 at a large kitchen supply store. It's also perfect for slicing brownies, cakes, and quiches, because they don't stick to the plastic blade.

Paper Plates and Cupcake Liners

For just a moment, try to think of a paper plate as a tool instead of a piece of disposable dinnerware. You can sift dry ingredients onto it, then lift and fold slightly to create a pouring spout. It's also handy for filling your pepper mill with those tiny peppercorns that have a tendency to roll in every direction. The cupcake liners can be used instead of prep bowls when measuring out small amounts, making pouring and cleanup easier.

Silicone Brushes

These little gems are such a great invention! No more stray "hairs" on your food from the old-style pastry brushes. You'll use these for brushing egg washes onto dough or basting meats with sauces. There are many different sizes from which to choose. Don't throw away your old-fashioned pastry brushes, though. They are useful in cleaning flour dust from your mixer parts.

Timer

I have to confess I can't cook without one. I suppose it's a throwback to my restaurant and bakery days. As good as my nose was in discerning when something was truly done, I was too much of a multitasker to cook without the backup of a good kitchen timer. Some of the digital timers that are available now even have the ability to time two different dishes at once.

Tongs

I love my spring-loaded tongs. They are great for turning or transferring meats without puncturing, but they are also useful for sautéing vegetables. Think of them as heatproof fingers. The spring-loaded tongs store easily, but if you don't have this type, use the cardboard tube from a roll of paper towels for easy storage. Cut off about 2 inches of the tube and insert the end of the tongs inside before storing in a drawer.

Wire Whisk

Whisks are available in many sizes and shapes, and you'll probably want an assortment for different uses. If you purchase only one, I would suggest a large, round balloon whisk for the basics. I tried for years to use a fork in place of a whisk, but I discovered it was well worth the investment to have this handy tool. There is nothing that can compare when trying to prevent lumps in custards, gravies, or sauces.

a well-equipped kitchen

Here are a few suggestions to consider when stocking your kitchen with implements and cookware.

My Favorite Piece of Kitchen Equipment
I would have to say that my KitchenAid stand mixer is my most treasured piece of kitchen equipment. It comes with a paddle attachment for cookie and pastry dough, a whisk attachment to beat cream and egg whites, and a dough hook for kneading bread dough. If you don't own one, I suggest you start saving. They are not inexpensive, but I can't imagine cooking or baking without one. Purchase the largest residential model you can afford (with at least a 5-quart mixing bowl).

Pots and Pans
Invest in a small set of heavy-bottomed stainless-steel saucepans, with matching lids, in at least three sizes: 1-quart, 2-quart, and 3-quart.

A Dutch oven for soups and stews is useful, and consider adding at least one small and one large skillet. If the large skillet is deep, it can be used for deep-frying as well as sautéing.

Baking Pans
My suggestion for baking pans is to purchase heavy, durable, rimmed aluminum baking sheets (also known as half sheet pans). Most inexpensive baking sheets warp when exposed to temperatures over 300°F. So no matter how economical they may appear in the beginning, they won't last. It's also a good idea to measure your oven before making a purchase. A good rule of thumb is to allow 2 inches of room on each side of the pan for air to circulate.

I don't recommend nonstick baking pans. Oils have a tendency to build up on the surface over time, leaving a sticky film on the pan that then affects the appearance and flavor of the foods you're preparing.

A basic arsenal of baking pans would include:

- 9 by 13-inch pan
- Three 8-inch square or round pans
- Three half sheet baking pans
- 7 by 10-inch jelly-roll pan
- Two 12-cup standard-size muffin pans
- Three 12-cup mini muffin pans
- Two jumbo-size muffin pans
- Two 9-inch pie pans
- Two 5 by 9-inch loaf pans
- Tube pan for angel food cake
- Bundt pan
- 9-inch round springform pan

Baking Dishes

You'll notice throughout this book that I suggest using "baking dishes" more often then baking pans. It is true that using a ceramic or glass dish, in place of a pan, can affect the way a product browns in the oven. But I like the fact that baking dishes make a nicer presentation than metal pans when brought to a table or buffet. They also keep me from having to transfer the food to a more presentable

serving platter, which cuts down on the cleanup. I've just become familiar with how to adjust my cooking time using this option, which really is minimal anyway.

Therefore, I suggest stocking up on different sizes of glass and ceramic baking dishes. I have a wide assortment, some rectangular, some oval, some square. I use my pie plates and 9 by 13-inch baking dishes the most, though.

Bowls

I have a set of four glass mixing bowls in graduated sizes. They come with lids that make them perfect for storing leftovers. I like it that they are microwave, oven, freezer, and dishwasher safe.

It's also nice to have both a very large metal bowl (with a capacity of at least 12 cups) and a very large ceramic bowl (with a capacity of at least 8 cups) for mixing larger quantities of foods.

Lastly, you would be amazed at the number of times you would use ceramic ramekins if you had them on hand. They make great prep bowls and condiment bowls and are especially nice for storing small amounts of leftovers.

timeless tips

Now that my children are getting older, it seems I often think of things I wish I had taught them as we made our early journey together. Thankfully, I have few regrets about how we have spent our time together and I have so many things to be happy about. But, if I only had a few hours to share my best <u>kitchen</u> wisdom with them before they leave the nest, these would be among my favorite little bits of advice.

Microwave Tip

Instead of using a piece of plastic wrap to cover your dish before microwaving, use a damp (but not soaking wet) paper towel to cover the dish. The paper towel won't collapse or melt onto the food, and it allows a good amount of steam to escape. It also prevents spattering and steam burns.

Slow Cooker Tips

- Brown meats and poultry in a skillet on the stove top before adding them to the slow cooker. This enhances the flavor, adds some color, and renders some fat.

- Because root vegetables are slow to cook through, always cut them into pieces no larger than 1 inch and put them in the bottom of the cooker so that they are surrounded by hot liquid.

- Use the low setting for tougher cuts of meat.

Organizing Tips

I'm kind of neat to a fault sometimes. I have a habit of storing almost everything out of sight because I just don't like clutter and I enjoy having a big workspace free of unnecessary objects. Sometimes this ordinarily good habit of stowing things away can come back to bite me, because I can't always remember where I put it!

But here is a list of storage ideas (that I actually _can_ remember) that might be helpful to you:

Dish brushes and vegetable scrubbers: Store them inside your dishwasher silverware basket. That way, they are out of sight, but in a great place to ensure a regular washing.

Spices: No, alphabetizing your spices does not make you an obsessive person! Find a way to do this, either on a shelf inside your cabinet or in a drawer with a spice divider. It will possibly keep you from purchasing a second, unnecessary jar of some expensive, obscure spice (that you only use once a year).

Trash bags: Store extras right in the bottom of the trash bin underneath the bag that is currently in use.

Tablecloths: I hang them in my closet on clothes hangers to keep them wrinkle free.

Cleaning Tips

I'm a clean-as-I-go cook. It just makes sense to me. So, I would break cleaning tips into two categories: As You Go (while you're preparing) and As You Can (a deeper cleaning that can only happen once in a while).

As You Go

- While baking or prepping, use waxed paper on the counter for easier clean-up. It provides a place for spoons and spatulas to rest. It's there to collect eggshells, vegetable peelings, flour dust, etc.

- When spraying a baking dish or skillet with nonstick cooking spray, hold it over the open door of your dishwasher to keep the "overspray" from landing on counters, floors, etc.

- Keep a glass shaker bottle full of baking soda near the kitchen sink, and as you notice stubborn spills, spot-clean them in an instant with just a quick shake. Baking soda, when combined with a small amount of water into a paste, is also very effective in cleaning stubborn places on cookware.

As You Can

- When using the self-cleaning option on your oven, place your outdoor grill racks inside the oven as well.

- For really stubborn stains, try using toothpaste on them. It usually works without ruining the finish on your appliances or countertop.

- Add a few small pieces of lemon or lemon rind to a microwave-safe measuring cup filled with water. Microwave for 4–5 minutes and then allow the lemon water to sit inside for 10 minutes more. Carefully remove the lemon water and pour it down the garbage disposal side of your sink. Wipe down the microwave. Then run the disposal for 30 seconds with cold water. You just got a good head start on cleaning both appliances, with that uplifting lemony scent as a bonus.

- I have a wonderful friend I don't get to see very often (Sheila!). She would designate certain days of the week for unpleasant tasks and strictly forbid herself to be bothered by them on any other day. For example, there was Worry Wednesday (she would only worry on Wednesdays) and Tidy Friday (she would only do deep-cleaning projects on Fridays). Follow Sheila's example and clean your refrigerator out every Friday (or the day before your trash pickup day). Bring those leftovers front and center, and use them or lose them. This gives you a chance to also take a quick inventory for that shopping list that needs to be written.

My Best Advice—In or Out of the Kitchen

Be thankful in all things. Be creative with what you have. Love one another. Tell the truth. Don't hurt someone on purpose. In the gaps between the good things that happen in life, the places where disappointment lives, work with the intention to fill in the spaces with forgiveness and grace. And, of course, make time to gather at your table.

Index